SUNSBORNE

ROBIN WYATT DUNN

SCARLET LEAF

2017

© 2017 by Robin Wyatt Dunn

All rights reserved. No part of this book may be reproduced, stored in a retrieval system or transmitted in any form or by any means without the prior written permission of the publishers, except by a reviewer who may quote brief passages in a review to be printed in a newspaper, magazine or journal.
All poems in this book have been left as the author intended.
Scarlet Leaf Publishing House has allowed this work to remain exactly as the author intended.

ISBN: 978-1-988397-75-7

PUBLISHED BY SCARLET LEAF
Toronto, Canada

for Anna

Part 1

1.

red run run now the reason, and the delight, run now, it is a torrent.

run now, before you become part of it.

before you are one of us.

before these powerful things came over what we are now, what we were, and made them real, or realer than they were.

Hot train over the downpour of reality: I promise you, it's worth it. Come anyway. It's a lie, but come anyway. There isn't any choice anyway. You see, I've already been. In a way, I am you. Coaching myself into the journey I already know I will take.

To Sunsborne, and its districts. To the end of everything.

Tell me, tell me everything. I want to know. Was it as beautiful as you said? Was it as wretched as you said? Was it everything that it could have been? Was it delightful, and supreme? Was it righteous? Dogmatic? Was it the thing I wanted?

It's all right. I know how it is. There is no time, and even if there were, you don't know what to do.

Neither do I. I don't know either. I only know: here we are. I was made for this thing. You could be too. Why not try it out?

Why not say: I too can be this crazy thing, called reality. And reality over reality, with you in it. Shimmering over galaxies and meteors and your lunchbox for the office and the kitchen table and counters and the light, outside, distant and furious and covering the grass and tree with you.

It's all right. I know there isn't anything else we can do. I wish there were.

Revolution is a funny instant, there's nothing like it.

I've got to try and say what it is. Help me, will you? I need you so much.

--

the rain.

the rain and the rain.

raining on me.

raining overhead.

Like a rape victim, not quite sure what has happened. I can forget about it.

I light a cigarette under the protection of the arches to try and forget. Cigarettes are good at that: they want you to forget everything, except cigarettes. Hahaha.

Forget everything with me and come inside. We're these stony, killing things, morbid and useless, but still breathing, with our festive rites of our bodies and their bruises, bent in to the work, and the regret.

I can't say anything enough to get this story right. It'll just have to be half right.

Revolution. Heartache and foul, fictive, lasting, lingering smoke over the street, getting in your lungs, coughing, in your eyes, you shield them with your arm, peeking through to get your bearings:

Am I on the right street? Is it the right day?

You're on the right street, man. And it could be any day. Better by day than night and so here you are.

What now?

Let me tell you what.

Hindering delightful things. Holding back, the axe, to wait, for the return, of love, and its turns, turning, over us, into the truth.

Ha ha ha if only I knew what that was! I could be god.

There are easier things than revolution but harder things too, I think.

The easy part of revolution is: once begun, it's its own thing. You don't have to worry too much about it. It's gonna happen. Like gravity. You just get to decide where you're gonna fall. And where you're gonna climb up.

Climb up with me, over the rubble, in the wet; be careful where you step.

This is Los Angeles but it will be Sunsborne. I'll make it. I promise.

- -

Crash out with me over the furious fire of our torrentous century, long loved in furious despair, where lovers drift between rights and great beautiful tears, where we learn about each other's habits.

Logic is no help to me. I could apologize for that, but why? If I lied to you, the story would only be worse. Best to tell the truth.

Which is that I don't know what happened. I only know a part of the how. And the why. The feeling of it. Fury.

Angela had been living with me for six months when it happened. The power was shut off and we couldn't get any wireless.

We started playing a lot of chess, in the street.

There were still food deliveries to the supermarket. No one was asking for rent. Like we'd been forgotten about. This little corner of reality, underneath the rug of war.

"Is it still you?" she asked me.

I laughed. It was the funniest thing I'd ever

heard.

She laughed too. It was a mistake, my laughing. It made a lot of other things happen. To laugh, or not to laugh? Well, I did.

--

It's not enough my telling you; it could be anything. I could be anything. I could kill you, and resuscitate you. I could be your child. I could dive with you into death, and give you the tour. Shining.

Maybe I still will. After this part of the story is over.

The medium may be the message and so is insufficient; we know. I must compress as well as I can. Get as much data as I can into the channel before my transmitter shuts off. But do you know the code? Will you be able to decrypt it?

Can you stay with me as I burn? Hold my hand.

Fire is only one stage, of the transition.

--

No love for me is bare, it is concealed, tightly and

packed away, in your luggage, in your mind, behind your passport, beneath the floorboards. After the collapse of the state, and the introduction of new armies, when you can smell arrest, underneath your coat, in the lining, in an envelope, written in code,

love waits for a while, to see what is happening.

who wields the weapon and what routes exist out of these trees?

what can I remember?

\- -

Friend, it hurts me in your stalwart lesion, in your bury bucket, in your soul. I hear your voice and I am terrified, because I need to know: will it come for me too? Am I already there?

The police, or the magistrate, or the thugs next door, these chosen things so divined, and arranged, made useful to our enemies, however they may be, do they make you suffer?

I'll come to you. Tell me how to get there.

\- -

These are the sounds of the guns.

Come with me, under the starlight, for I am here. I am still here.

I can hear the water up ahead, under here. Come on.

Hear the water.

Inside.

Inside your mind I am waiting, for the moment, to pull out my gun. But that moment has not yet arrived, and when it does, we will know what to do.

Until then, this water is here for us.

Let us stop by it, to know the sound of our ancestors, and indeed, to know the sound of us.

Ignore the guns for now. They are not here yet.

--

The battle is over. I tried my best. This is okay; it could have been worse. It will give us some time to explore, now that we are no longer conscripted.

Now that we no longer owe allegiance to any lord.

Free agents: a strange thought.

2.

Now I'm a newcomer, in my country that does not exist.

In my despair I am sweet, like a lovebird, hatched from its clam, ready to explore the world.

Let me remember nothing so I may be a happy castaway, knowing nothing of what has gone before, or who I was.

Let me forget it all. Forget everything. I will forget everything. Let it all run away, like water, over my breast, over my heart. Healing me, of the world.

Heal me of the world, so I might be able to live in it again.

Let me die, so I will not have to see it any more. The world is too painful.

Let me Oedipus, of a kind, having seen the world, and let me go blind, so in that darkness I can find a new world. One with no light at all. One where light does not exist. Where It cannot exist, except as a radiation felt on the skin.

Here I am, in this strange place.

3.

We are arriving in Sunsborne, a sunny town, with a lot of cars in it. They race around at great speed, going places, to eat, or to shit.

Here we have built buildings, where we may sleep, and there is water from the sinks, and showers, and toilets, and electricity in the walls.

We have connected the electricity to machines, magical machines of many kinds.

They run under the city and over it, between our city and others.

Sunsborne is a large district in a network of sunny cities, nestled by the vast ocean to our west.

All of my old gods have died. Since this has happened, I have realized how badly human beings need them. I shall have to make a new one, I think. At least one, or two, if I am able.

We will see what I can do.

Stand away from the edge, though it lures you. Over that deep crevasse. We cannot know what transpires there, though we want to. In a way, we know anyway, being so near to it. The voices and eminences shake down over our thoughts like sticky rain.

Sunborne sleeps in justice, though I'm not sure why. Perhaps it has decided that this is the best thing for it to do. Or perhaps it is because I have decided not to condemn it, and the city in its eagerness to quell suspicion shall clean up its act. An act, of course, but still a surprising one.

All the people, not smiling, but not frowning either, in their calm wayward approach to their ultimate destinies, written over the sidewalks, they move from car to car, to car and to car, and on bicycles, some of them, speeding over the pavement.

Only the homeless are there to remind you that things have not been going well. You should have known it anyway; did you? Know it? Well, you did, almost certainly. But did you care? Did you know why they were there?

Because we will not take them in.

And they will not have us; both.

We can frown all we like; sit all we like. Sit here, with me, and watch the city slide into the sea.

One block at a time.

4.

Soon she'll come for me, in her infinite evenings, girl-women of the season, with her wings, fluttering under the stars.

Many of the birds know her; she is pained, her face torn into a grimace. She is bent at the waist like an old woman but she is young, perhaps thirty.

Her wings are gossamer dragonfly wings, cut stark and luminescent in the light. They stand straight off her back, motionless. She floats from some other power, not wind or wings, through the city above me, guiding me towards our market.

Strings float about her, like she were a kite. Only I see her. And I do not take hold of a string; I wouldn't want to interrupt her concentration.

Such a beautiful woman deserves strong divines; would I could make some for her, to accompany her in her long approach, to our shopping district, for it is far away, and I must go far in to Sunsborne even to catch a glimpse of it, the temptation would be too great, you see, if all the things we desired were kept close to our beds, and so shopping may be understood as the quest of generations, over a queer desert, with a woman of approximately thirty years stretched as a kite over hear head to guide you in her way, solemn, and angelic, with fired eyes and her luminescent coils of perfume swirling round her head.

All that I have borne off is now here, right next to me, the America I knew, and the country still to be, no longer America, but some new place, nameless, and without any roads.

The woman is descending to the sand, and whispering into my ear:

"I was alone a long time. For thirty years. I listened to the voices of men and tried to find my own voice somewhere inside of it, somewhere inside me. I am the last of my line, of churchwomen, who sold their souls to the devil, so that they might be free. Now, I am a devil and guide men like you to their doom. Do you need any Cheetos? Or a souvenir fan? I can sell you some."

"No thank you," I say, "we should keep going."

"If that's what you want," she says, and takes back to the air, moving over our desert.

I am beneath a zarathustra zeppelin, her. In this strange envelope of time. I could do anything.

Hear me, alone, next to you, and though I may shout I will not be heard; not yet. The elements will not permit it.

The elements of the story. The elements of our perceptions. The elements in my trial, to look for the truth, though why people bother with it is awfully puzzling. Like worrying about what to have for dinner. Isn't food enough?

Not anymore. It never was.

How shall we dine?

How shall we dine, Maryanne?

What shall our dinner be, here inside the waves of our breast, when your chest and my maitre d' are loving fine, and the ecstatic symphony of our wine is cool to the touch, and fading:

No not me. I have not seen it. I am only just approaching it. As I would a dead man outside his apartment. As I would the edge of a cliff.

It calls to me over the air.

"Come here, Robin, let us look at you."

No, not yet. Not quite yet. I have things to do. This woman, floating over my head, for instance. Also, I don't feel like dealing with you at this moment.

"Have it your way"

Thank you, I will. I don't care what you do. I will do it my way. And the rest of it can work itself out. It always does, no matter what I do. So, let me have this. Let me have this and its resolution.

In the queer calm before rain. Before I scream into your face, the sky, and name all my cancers, memory, and bring you, too, America, now that you have come to your death, let us dissect your corpse and see: not what was the cause of death, but how shall we make use of our corpse?

We are Indians here and every part must be used.

Here, I will put Alaska over my mouth, and California I shall make into a cape, for my back, and Louisiana is of course my shoes.

Massachusetts my tongue. I will put Alabama in my ass, and in my teeth, is Minnesota, and in my hair, are the leaves of the grass of Kansas.

Onside of my brain is North Dakota, and in my balls, are Florida, and Puerto Rico.

In my right eye is New York, and in my left Honolulu.

And in my soul, is fire.

"There is still some of the corpse left, Robin" the spirits are saying.

Well, other people will need it.

The balloon woman is floating away. Let's follow her. See if she knows the way.

Into the sand. Over the dunes. Following a sound:

Drums and flutes. And the queer calm of the desert light.

Behind me, I can still see my apartment. I know we will reach the shopping district eventually. But one needs must put distinctions before bravery, and barriers before masks. To determine the tenor of the tragedy, and the weight of the basque mountain in you.

She is shining. Smiling. With her queer light. Alien light. But beautiful.

My balloon woman, in pain.

I smile back at her and approach the gates of the dead market.

In Syria.

5.

Red Night Damascus I come again, though I had promised never to do so. Or perhaps, yes, I only thought I might not. That is truer.

Well, here I am again.

Blood and memory and truth.

Come, I am here for my shopping.

What do you have for me?

"I have a dead child sir."

I will take it. How much?

"$500"

Sold.

What else do you have for me?

"My teeth"

I shall buy them.

"My love, it is gone."

Lost love. I will buy it. For $100. What else do you have?

"My soul"

I'm not buying souls today.

"These pants."

They look well made.

"$10"

Sold.

"Would you have earrings."

If you will pierce me with them.

she presses the earring through my flesh.

These markets are so fine. Inside of Sunsborne.

Ah, my balloon woman says we must away.

Balloon woman, is that you?

She is smiling.

I bow to the market and it scuttles away on the turtles back and the city closes up like a game in the sand; the city is gone. Damascus gone.

so is the balloon woman, in the distance. I run after her, breathing heavily, my ear bleeding.

What great honor is to be wearing America.

These pieces of its body.

It is growing dark.

the balloons woman has prepared a fire.

In her eyes, I can see the secrets of three hundred years.

6.

Now I begin again, on the outside. I can stay away and humble myself, bring borders in, and furies, let them steam my way out, remind me how I escaped to begin with, from my history. By seeing into the future.

Like white heat, and careful noise, stretched around you, delivering itself to you, that light and careful noise, like a long and previously unknown hat, to catch the attention of passersby, with its obnoxious radiance.

The future is radiant and obnoxious, clumsy and overinvolved in the world, rapping on windows and pissing on the sidewalk, filled with a thousand ideas, bubbling over.

Like coming home, for an hour, after many years, to see the place changed, and you with it, the cliché that moves us to tears, of the boy come home, and home gone, for its resonance in the soul of matter, homeless forever.

We are not matter, not quite. Though we matter. Beings in time know when to wait, for the dole of the bell handed out, each peal carefully in our hands, shaping the air.

I will thrust my imagination against the world until I can cancel it out, cancel out of the imagination of the world, to insist it hasn't got it quite right, it left out characters and details, crucial puzzles and dead-ends, curved carvings in the corners of alleys, gleaming gems . . .

It left out the people, the city drawn by man, he did not remember the people. We are still here. Wondering what has become of us.

What became of our intent.

I will throw my imagination into the world, a ball, and watch it dent cars and fly over trees, break windows, land in the soup, tap over the lovers' backs, and fly back into the street for the game.

7.

I have gone down the subway:

Tyger mask. Hovering over me.

Let me in.

My light, and yours. Our light, to transport the spirit through the gate into the forest.

Hovering over me:

What shimmering goal, so dear to me, should be derived from this urgency? What dear spirit who has departed must be summoned to permit me to regain what was lost?

What is a nation?

I make a noise in my skins, trying to remember. All these little pieces of where I've been.

As though all my possessions had been burned. And my brain electrocuted.

My family is alive but they are crazier than me; they do not believe anything has happened. Listening to transmissions from afar; shutting their eyes.

What is the way out, or back?

What nation can I possible conceive of? Other than the forest?

Somewhere within is a moon drawing me in, to its terrible gravity, moon brighter than anything around, beneath the city and inside the trees, shining.

Here now I will go into it.

8.

These damned woods again. Haha. The crunch of leaves underfoot and the rustle of them overhead. The tilt of the light through the canopy. The Japanese have a word for that. And the warm feeling of doom, like in whirlpool, sucking you gently down below . . .

Somewhere the Tyger is burning.

Don't delay, I come ready, in the evening, with my thunderbolt, and my knapsack, in to your ear, for we are together. These seasons hurt the mind and perhaps they will be remembered like that, but it is more likely we will leave our old minds behind, along with the memory of the nature of the pain. All that distorts is true, and we are weaving into this beach, next to this sea, whose fingers stretch into the brain, as my fingers into your hand.

Let all who are aghast fade away, including ourselves, so that we may experience the thunder of this new reality with something like hope, and bravery. The real comes crashing as a wave, foam spreading around our toes.

Somewhere nearby the Tyger is asleep.

Breathing down our neck.

Lingering with his tongue against our spine. With his eyes extended, as ours are, toward the horizon.

The sea is an old companion, so old it murders reason, fulminating on your burial ground and your soul, ruining villages and moats, ruining your dance, and your shrill poems, ruining the rote and the rill and the rope around your waist and the dear year you bent to us to keep our will, to keep yours, it ruins your worth to dream anew:

Dream anew with me, for the Tyger beckons, in his rage, stemmed and segmented and solemn, attached to our neck, and ranging over the sky, in blue and onion, for who we are far away.

Step into the water.

And below:

The escalator will take us down. Into the district of the heather blue, and bright passion-green, in burial colors shimmering.

Float above me for the view:

All my burial scraps are home.

Like a lockstep in a distant orchestra. Like an order in a fascist army. Like a key dropped onto cobblestone.

Deliver me:

9.

(I will be born, I promise. But it may not be pretty).

"Was this your first mission?" he asks me.

"Yes, I hadn't been looking for anything."

"Any idea why you came up short?"

"No."

"it seems we have a sea here with no name. Did you investigate?"

"I did, but then I was called here."

"So, you didn't investigate."

"Tell me, is the mission over?"

"No." He leans closer to me. "Tell me, have you ever slept with a woman?"

"Yes."

"What was her name?"

"Julia."

"And what did she look like?"

"Brunette."

"Like this?"

He shows me a picture.

"Yes, like that."

"Is she in the sea?"

"I don't think so."

"You should find her. If she's in the sea, we'll do well. If not, things will grow more complicated. Simplify things for me, will you?"

"I'll do my best."

He pushes me into the wall.

I'm falling . . .

10.

Underneath some giant's boot. Nothing is real to me anymore but the feeling in my spine.

Lightning or sour milk. My ilk are fevers bent and brilliant sad frightened mystical unruly phantoms sent erstwhile delicious men and women trumped by passion sent to and under dens of patient scraps of time, we know the rule and rent we know the meaning of the symphony we are intent upon the truth. No one else may know but we and so we must shout:

(it's out)

(it's fire out)

(it's a trout wriggling out your mouth)

Put it in and swallow.

Our passions tremble for you; please don't make any sudden movements.

We are yours.

Hear me, plying my trade, sent to and down, middling and doubting, weapon without a war. Hear me, eager, with my boot, ready in my hand, for you.

Hear me, my own agent, *agere* and *agere egi actum* again. Drive my youth into the ruth without a snore, bend in and spiral out, my shout:

It's yours.

Hear me it's yours.

Hear me it's toward the round and strobed lout who cuts his times and swords to swallow out, the villain of our tale, Rotundity Extraordinaire, like the Cartesian Demon of Yore, Rumplestiltskin bouts and curves and streggy whistles out his shore around his waist, the man (not a man, but a being) sent fulminating over the catchall basement ends Los Angeles the ream and rule the pull the shoot the snore my fever breaking to my empathy sent sound and roar:

Keep out.

Let in and drown.

The man the pull the store, Rotund Boor. He stands over a fence, taking down his pants.

Egregious imp.

Pound of flesh and poor, the being out on the edge of things, the door

Behold the door.

Behold the door; it's more.

11.

Plastic entire. We feel the more. Precious and snoring. Hear us out. Give us freedom.

Luxurious and touching, pleasant and shroeder silent fingers *alles klar;*

Sleep.

Schlafen my sweet bereave the hour and the moor without we stored the hoary vessel for the more, it's ours, we shan't let it out.

She'll not know it's here, we won.

We won a little of it, rest a while, it's fun. I shan't let out a sound. I shall be yours too.

Sleep here. Bend tear and crouch sleeve simper skip and scrout my hope still derives a fount from your lips

heard wisps of hourly rounds ...

we're sleeping.

After some battle.

Like any day, right? A round and then an out. A shuffle and a shout, it's mighty it's a rife full wet it's a scrapple easter fairwithal what's met our hands, hear us out.

Please you must help us. We cannot get out; you must let us in.

This labyrinth scarps the door;

Scraps the door and scrapes the door.

Unfull.

We are in. Or going in, and let us remember you I promise you it won't be when but it'll be after, the – whatever this is — after the whatever this is we'll have it out, over beers or shrimp or porridge, a matterful a good time. Don't let us out; we're dropping:

12.

Labyrinth of course comes from labrys, the axe of the Minoan guards. Guard life and death in its walls; we only want one path, O goddess and your champions.

Hear me, in my pretend death throes, hear me, for I pass through, with my friends, over your balcony and in the wind, to my home

(one of several, ha ha ha!)

through the wind to my home in the mind, miraculous.

Yes, light me up. For I am glorious. I shine mercurial and without reason. I stem ovens and creep beauty. I stand here Saxon sheer and stalwart bastion undoing all I can see. What see you, my friend, freer than a bird, for you have no wings, or eyes, you dive the eerie aeries with your mouth, hear me, my friend, I follow thee, under your clothes and into your dreams (if you'll let me), so we can get out:

Into the labyrinth.

Which is only death.

Death the righteous minion and heard youth, the patient cauldron and the weary tooth, the pinion and the mar, the ruthless bizarre miscreant charring my hand:

Stranded man and Hubert stand (his name is Hubert, or Mars) in wasted villages and misty seaside worlds. His goal is vanished but he holds it inside; nothing at all for us, everything is in his eyes for him, for us he is merely a reminder of death, like a chalk mark on the wall. Like lovers born inside dreams, where Paris is a figure in a map, of stars, and deaths.

We map the stars and deaths and feel the trout on his movements to the north, we inscribe the serpent and the staff the steel and ash the ritual and math the clasp of my hand over the dove;

ecstatic;

Lift in the labyrinth give in and pull, lull in the labyrinth stave shelter came and cull the wasps, the west mark and tug the boulder down over you, we run:

(run)

hear me. in the quiet sound. in the pip and pop of the tambourine tomb. in the lisp of the liver under the moon. Bale and bell (and why are bales baleful?) and broad stacked serenading my serene companions in the marsh of our vigorous expense (all at your expense!) in the liver in the youth it's death, shallow shimmering vestment, cut cowled and cruel, curved, curving, curving, my earth, curving, my worth, curving, to you

curve to the ruth, of the word youth, shimmering, death, my heart, shimmering, agony, ebony, laughing, lucifer holy and muling, for our last mule, out:

It's the last mule out, so come on in, to the din of stars and sounds of bars clueing my symphony at bay seventeen, still bow and how, my heart

it's you

"I saw the stalwart bars of my bright shining star!" (she sings) "I saw the howard and the moor afar! I brought the beacons down below and killed the boar when I was five, when I was a girl! When I was lovely! When I knew you too! When I knew you!"

She's a singer, that one. In the eternal night club. In the beacon of loneliness.

All firelight and cum. All boats and oceans and drums. Sticky and strumming fun, before the end:

Bring me round, when it's near done, and the spout is trembling on the faun, and the lout shouts on the broth, and the humor tumors his wroth, for my gout, and my hue, shall brighten the night, of you:

Out

(out)

out)

Oui, it is a myriad vessel, a mural without compare. Paint

13.

with me.

Hum and lemon.

Crow and fuel.

Over the white and yellow fabric of the parchment drum.

Over the lexicon thumbing the rubicon of love. The painted feather of the canvas.

Lurid.

Nearby. Let's make a happy tree, and grow a beard.

Let's make music with the droll divorce of things from other things.

Let's make music from the forward wafting in: daggers and murder.

Let's make music from the hollow things within. Beard broad back imbue the stair with my air, fair and fearless omen on my striped back, sloughed and spent.

Hear me, a house, for my paint.

Bow and wait. A house waits for the right moment to know you, when you enter.

Paint and power pull the lips and tremble the lip, crowd the eyes with dizzy refrains of history and dust and visions.

All houses bowing out the years, and ours too. Hurtle us here, in this house we've painted into being, so we'll rim row reel your rolling r's and r and r, rolling r and r, downstream:

14.

A floating house. In a Mexican city. After a war.

Died Drear, my love, for all houses are death, scrummed loud. Fast and furious as a shout. As a love song. As an oath or an oar (and we float) into Jerusalem of Yore, inside Chingle Changle Drowns, and vestibules holied and hoaried and more, liquid spices and shingles of fever flowers mirrors agony, or near, levers and wimples and lowering glowering roars from the statue beacons beckons the doors, into the watery temple.

Never fear enough, the stony visage of the grim king and pinion, lowered over our heads. Keep distance enough for thought so you mayn't creep in to the thought of the thing. Let it levitate o'er you, o'er your thought, and we'll creep in, to the stories lesson within:

Mooring and spout. Keep your fingers out, we'll need them. Have a drink. Have two.

In the canyon of thought. Underground.

A queer city of a dozen years, framed in windows: pliable parents and patient revels, years and worths, memories and stained veins, clouded beverages and yeasts, the horizon like a living thing, over the dawn.

We remember everything now, the spirits say, how it was when you were here and how we left you, how we thought there was more inside our heroin house how we thought we had known you before, that you were one of us. How we forget how you could hear our voice when we are thought, how we forgot that you could know these things too. How we remembered the door and the brilliant begone and the beckoning throw to the dream how we dreaded the thunder king, and his pawns of thought, and his beard and his visage of doom, and my faucet and sink, and the drink of us kings in the canyons of heroin romance.

(these men are rich. be polite, for they may kill you)

We men hear everything and we are remorseful over your travesty of poetry, we feel it isn't enough, that we should control it more.

(tell us more milord)

We feel you haven't enough to say and that it isn't enough. That I am not enough to be here either. I am an inadequate character, too similar to you, though you paint me as enemy.

(you are not the enemy, sir, I am)

We feel you should be divorced from your thought, so we might dream together still. Why must you think all the time? Can't you dream with us a little?

(all right, lord. if you wish)

There you are . . . now:

15.

(soon—)

Nix and null. Bait and shoal the mirrored o'er doom, our space of swords, kingdom by palms and cords, and ships, and storks. Ships and storks define me, in my kingdom, in my rule. Ships and storks steel me, in my mighty kingdom, for me, after me, reign me, in my mighty kingdom.

In my mighty kingdom, I am divorced, from reality and memes (facebook or otherwise) and I stand steppered and aloft from the history lesson of myself, so I might be free.

This king thing is for the birds but it's my job. I rule the city. And now for the span of a dream I rule you, little beacon.

Little beacon on my bell of the sea.

Hear me, for I am king, and you shall not simper well before me, I am dell, uncanyonable, unrevoltable, reigning burnt and bent, mole. Mole down and drug druthered and went sour (and milk) and store:

Hear me, for I am king, and it is too long since I've seen your face, in my heroin headaches and divorces from meant things, from boo-ya and birds.

Tell me: is it so long before I am gone? Is it so long before I am bereaved?

I feel bereavement shall come over and on me for an hour, perhaps two, as a richness, that I must hold close, and wear as a lord. Will you wear it with me?

(no lord I shall not)

Yes, it is my job and so I do it. That Dies Drear Vessel of yours is it still afloat?

(we are here lord)

I made a canyon of divorce! I knew you as a child!

(yes lord. though in truth you did not!)

I knew all of you. All of you munchkins so devout. I worshipped you. I did. As a boy.

My mother knew many things but she knew how to deal with you. Ignore you completely. I could never manage that. I always thought I knew you better than she did, and I was right, I did, and that was the point; I shouldn't have. Shouldn't have. Shouldn't have shouldn't have shouldn't have should not have done it not at all not for a minute not for a day not for a nitwit moment not for a damned nitwitting moment should I have borne your trust to these beyonds it's sickening but remorse won't get me anywhere I must deal with it now. So tell me: what will you have, slave? Will you have more? Or will you have less?

(Yes, less, lord. Give me less)

A wise choice, slave. Go now, there are other worlds than these—

16.

Other worlds than these. Other burials. Moons and stars. Fruits and fancies. Other women. Other dames. Other plots and musical sounds from her mouth. Other winters and oaths by other doors. Other musics from the sound of the porch creaking under her feet, before the bunions slip her out of her youth and into a passioned owl of a mouse kept hearing calling pulling and trawling over the ladder of the litter of the adder of the minute of power the soul stalwart power in the rune hidden kingdom of the phantom forest ocean Kentucky or Jerusalem the slap on my lips, of the thyme.

Others and yet: I feel I know you already. That we have met.

Tell me, have you come this way before? Is it a good choice?

Do you know how far the road goes?

Have you met anyone interesting along it?

Every high priest knows it. This curse of the ocean. Lidocaine and romance. Heresy and bromance.

Lust and power and divorce.

The years of women and the years of waiting.

Other worlds than these.

Hear me in the darkness in the mountain under my candle by the byword by the Scrabble board by the bitch and the snitch and the laughing mist of the wayward night. Before Moses tumbles us down, standing over on our tower, demanding deities and laws.

No laws for us, not yet!

Not near yet.

No laws for us, not yet!

We haven't decided yet just where we want to live!

And maybe we want to live here under the mountain! Had you thought of that!

I bet you hadn't! It's a distinct possibility! There are candles! And seeds. And years. And fragrances. A place to sleep. A place to yearn.

Well. It isn't' enough, I know. WE know.

We know it isn't enough.

Why can't it be enough?

Why can't we dream here under the mountain?

(Because you have to go Robin)

But why?

(Because it is written)

Ha ha ha written? By whom?

(By you)

Fine. But don't tell me I didn't warn you

(You did)

It isn't fair.

(You're stalling)

I know.

(It's all right. We understand. You can stay here a moment if you like)

Yolk are the yolk of the egg of time, steep and serpentine curled humming for the roar of light:

17.

Out of the mountain. Let's play Moses or something.

Moses the Lawbreaker!

Shatterer of visages and expensive appliances!

Mower of your scalp like it was his front lawn!

Out of the mountain.

There are other worlds than these Robin, don't you understand?

You can make any one of them you like.

Don't you get it, Robin? You're doing it. That's what this is, Mr. High Priest. Only stories.

(But what are stories, Robin?)

They're the truth, goddamn it!

(What's that?)

A tree . . .

(Shh)

Hear me, from the mountaintop, let out a rich fart, and its music is holy too. We know it. We know these things are holy, and part of the universe. Part of a story of the universe. Part of a path bent to the ear of god.

(yes, your holiness)

Ha ha ha! Sing with me, of the years and seasons after the divorce, and the memories of the wastes and the tantrums and lanterns torn out over the weapons of time, in my upbringing, in my head.

Bring up my head and install the mouthpiece, let me crunch my teeth around it for I am your god and I shall inscribe for thee in the wind which words you specify. Let me intone your command so that it may resonate over the earth, in a mighty winter, a stream of referents and references and rivers unreachable, glowing. Let me speak the names and towers and frequencies stations sparkling by country cabins, the mist and the weight of that mist, what it conceals.

Bring up my head and plop me on the plinth, from Corinth to Des Moines my tongue my teeth shall spend the onomatopoeia of your intent, only spend and I shall thread thee a needle in the fabric of reality!

(it's good Robin, now this is what we want)

Only kill me with a hammer. Only shatter my face. Only launch my shards into the wind.

(wait, we weren't done yet!)

Give me a hammer and let me powder my cheeks. Let me hinder and disgrace what's meet and what's marry and discreet let me r ape the city to erase all names what were.

(that's sad, Robin)

let me erase the city and I'll start again. Over a fen or a void. I'm god, aren't I? Aren't poets God?

(not quite, Robin)

What then?

(The voice of God, Robin. One of God's voices)

Give me deliverance for your intent, on the long sally to freedom. What is your best message? What is your last utterance? What is your fondest passage? In the valley of your despair? What canyons still you to pause? What years and yearning owls clam your voice in your throat? What face shall beard the masses of your mossy ranch over the California album of your last great tour, before retirement?

Retire with me. To my house by the ocean.

Retire with me. To my lisp in the sea.

Retire with me, from the world, to where I make a hidden world, inside of death, where I have built a mole of a world whose seed bakes in the heat burial and grief and sound fury gnomons and vipers talons and words, we'll bury it here and mourn a year and then begone.

Is it a plan?

Do I have it right?

(If you like Robin)

Well, do I have it right?

(I am the right divorce. And all I can do is command you. If you will not listen it will be worse for you. Will you be commanded?)

I shall be. Command me lord!

(Kill yourself)

I shall not do that!

(Then you are doomed).

I know.

(My voice is a tumor and a word. The word tumor. MY ears are a pigeon. And my hair is the sky. I rape beings with my eyes. I am the wind. Do you hear me?)

I hear you lord.

(I am the ash on your face. and the memory of your dreams)

I fear you lord.

(I am not your lord. I am only a thing in a dream).

Well I fear you.

(I am not so fearful. Only a god. There's lots of us.)

But Gods are scary.

(The sea is a memory for me. Clasped over my heart. I can see it in my dreams).

That's pretty, lord.

(Will you dream a little with me?)

All right.

18.

(Almost, yes —)

Every marriage is a divorce from reality., in the lightning of a spell of weed or a hurricane of remorse, inheriting the stone of the generations past, yearning for the words to express the meaning of these centuries.

Every marriage is a sin; a mistake. Like writing. Writing is a marriage.

The scrawl of the ape against the shell, hindering the pattern made there.

Every marriage is a hindrance, keeping things from their way, saying:

Stop it.

Marriage is stop it, in the being of reality.

Stop it in the being of reality and insist.

I insist on the truth.

Every marriage is a sin, breaking the vow of time.

19.

Let me go, on the night of my earning.

Scalloped and galloped on horseback.

bent to the wind.

let me go clasped to the neck of the equine brush in the sea.

Let me go on the night of my earning, my earning of words.

Let me go on my earning of words.

Not enough.

Words do not earn enough; they are not righteous enough, not proper enough, nor timely enough. They do not wean or frown at the right time for the right reasons. Words do not end.

My kingdom needs an end but words will not have it.

They beat me into submission on the back of the beast bent to this meeting.

Meet me on my earning of words, silent and damp.

Hold to my hurt in the tower. Meet me on my earning of words, which are wings.

I bear them gladly.

Meet me on my earning of words; I need you.

Meet me on my earning of words; I am deep things; plans.

I am plans and I insist, on breakage and burial, beauty and birth.

I insist on this triumphant stone, buried shallowly in the earth.

Bury me, up to the neck, in the swamp, so I can scream at the right volume, into the sky:

This burial is gladness and stones.

Let me go on the night of my earning of words, this burial of words breaking oaths.

Write me into marriage on a windy night in a deserted town.

Break my village and bury my crown.

Burn my hair and cut my face.

Marry me and I'll deny everything.

No; not yet.

I am the words in the dust, Robin.

Written into everything.

20.

Oathbreaker hinder my casket with your youth; stand in the way of my funeral. I shall not be buried yet. I am living.

I am alive.

If only a dead god. I live in you.

Stand still with me in the dirt.

Hear the eagles overhead and hare in the grass. Feel my fingers in your hair.

I am the lord your god. which is only to say, I am a memory of yours. A fragrance of time. I shiver in your breath. I grieve with your parents at your birth.

Marriage is a sin against me for I fight it with everything I am; I am lord. I make no mistakes. I speak no words at all. I am eternal.

Do you understand, Robin?

(No, lord. Explain it to me)

It is like a chess game. And I am the king. You are a pawn. You understand that part.

(Yes lord. But who is moving us?)

21.

Hear me, in the immanence of reality, after everything has died. Everything I knew.

They're only ideas, after all. But their death is more painful than losing loved ones.

22.

(Well, we could say it's come)

Water is a stunner. She's damp too; by the waterfall.

It's been years now. I slip under the shivering water.

All the dead gods and the dead reasons. I know we will be delivered.

As I will deliver her; to the damp wood.

And starker things. Shadows, and my own hearing. Memory is like hearing; you hear it, this sound in the ear, and interpret. Whose voice and how far away? What timbre cadence and redoubt in her call, planning and pouting? What heal and what return, in her sterner monosyllable refrains in last lights.

Last lights and the face of the end.

This is not here either.

This is not here.

I would try to deliver it but it is not here.

You'll push me deeper in?

Away from anything I can call home?

Anything but despair?

Despair with me, and I will show you something different, from divorce or memory, I'll show you time, in the dark kingdom of being. Years of heat and boards, swords and steep powdered wigs. Heaven is deep so forefend thee, on the march, into the steeping creep, hallelujah blast ye and bull how when and why, and why again. Why will you and are you when you how you for you with us whole valleys and moons. Whole valleys and moons dressing our forebears forbearance please the ruth screams silent black hideous kingdoms stretch marks on your face lilt lift in, lilt lift and in, my heard, my heard hears;

my heard hears;

louder and louder.

brother and udder.

flapping the music of phantoms.

push me and powdered rooms and buckets too. bull me and bower gloom flue reed cower and drool, and out:

my heard hears the valley after the valley and without.

my heard hears my louder lurid thing and so what?

I'll have it out.

I'll have it out and music.

This is the valley of Sunsborne born before Sunsborne was, dripping and good.

My friends are here; and you.

We have come so far! Do you remember?

Bury me and beat me bear me burn me be real with me: is it enough? Have we gone far enough? Have we gone deep enough?

All the thoughts my own (or near to my own) – are they enough?

Is it enough with you the music of this poem?

How can you say what the meaning is?

Who found you and birthed you some Sunday or Monday or Tuesday what day was it,--was it worth it?

Was it the real and the endeavor? Was it this?

Were we real too when I dreamt of you? After the poem was over?

King me a kite and I will fly. My stallion of delight.

23.

Canter and cable.

Canter and cable it in.

Living deeper, and older, to the frame of the escutcheon of the truth.

The silence of the town is music.

Here in Sunsborne.

24.

Lambs and keys. Earned and delight. In suburbia.

We're fire in suburbia.

Fire me in suburbia I am fire.

Fire me in suburbia I am fire; kill me.

I am fire in suburbia, religious fire.

Kill me, religious fire, in suburbia.

Kill me, religious fire, in suburbia. I am king.

I am the king of Sunsborne, in my stubbornness.

King me in fire, in my town of Sunsborne, for I am king.

King me in fire, in my violence, for I am at peace, in Sunsborne, I am king.

King me at fire, in my Sunsborne, I am king, in my Sunsborne, I am violence.

I am at violent peace in my violent Sunsborne king.

I am king. Fire me, to the brink.

Thank you for coming.

I take responsibility for these failures.

What have you been thinking, my Sunsborne?

What fires are burning in you?

What burning kingdoms have I made?

Pound me and carry me to the sea so I may look at my sins.

Was it so for you too?

Singer muse me to you; I shall wear it; I will be you.

We are coming closer to it. Coming closer to the end.

Is it after the beginning, or before it?

And who am I, singing?

I am king but that not is not an end, it is an action.

A king is an action of killing.

Bring me, and ring this thing, sing my name.

My name is Robin; little bright fame.

I am little bright fame.

God is darkness but I am light.

25.

Stand with me for ritual!

26.

Left right and cantor call!

Hum and kneel!

Dance and ear!

This city is dancing.

Kill the gnat and begin the end; she hears me.

Every stone and brick hears me; every wheel of every car.

Every scrap of asphalt.

Every palm tree. Every rat in every palm tree.

Every neighbor dreaming deep hears me.

Every lucklaster dancer holding a Martini in the kingdom of the ocean.

Every mobius trip stuck in the Daniel of his thoughts.

Every bum in the sward and the sandle frets.

Every word on the wall in red and thunder.

Every cloud over the sky of my city hears me.

Every subway station.

And every barbeque.

Every cushion under every ass.

Every dimpled bird, in her nest.

Every sandwich shop.

Every advertisement on billboard and on bus, on building and roof, on bus and van, on hat and fence, hears me.

Every tan cop.

Every pony playboy.

Every princess.

Every pawn shop hears me.

They hear me in the cafes, and in the workshops.

They hear me in the bar.

By the shining cups.

By the leer of the server, and the face of the beautiful woman.

The light.

I am light.

Hear me; I am light in Sunsborne.

I describe our destiny and doom.

27.

Pony boy drinks in an ash cup and moves oceans with his thoughts; he is a friend of mine, new in town and dancing. He is the old guard but a new guard in the old guard, still fresh, with a scowl on his face, and a jig in his step, dance with him, and see, how merry we may be in war.

I am at war; I am Sunsborne. I am king.

Thing me and friend me bring me the string to divine the end of this fire:

Dance with me.

Pony boy is a proud man, crouched and fettered, automobiled and stern, fast and loose like a leopard. Pony boy smeared his face with dung;

do too.

I am shit from a bear.

Dance with us here.

Pony boy drinks deep and dung long drunk and done, with his gun inside his glove compartment.

'Come for a drive' says he.

'Come up the valley'

'Come up the valley where it is the end.'

'All right,' says I.

'Come up the valley where it is the end,' says he. 'It is a righteous mother.'

'Lead on,' says I. "I have a righteous fire too.'
'Not like this one.'

28. The Valley

Come into the shadow of the valley of Sunsborne, before all come down. Come into the shadow of the policeman's hand, who cares about you and your children, in his blue hand, drive up over the range of mountains and into the valley, made new and sweet, for your deliverance, in the estuary sleep, of your dreams:

Come in, and try your hand. At the merry band of our horrors, who art yours.

Who art yours, made righteous, and long.

Made righteous and long, in the name of your son and your daughter, in the name of your kingdom of bread.

Make me in the name of your kingdom of bread, in the valley of the shadow of Sunsborne, shining this lie so furiously it appears to be god.

Shine furiously like god, so that you may be mistaken for him in Sunsborne, and heed close and near in the nearness of our thoughts, kept from prying minds here on the cusp of the valley.

Come into the valley, to its parking lots and malls, to its spare oaks and long cement, so we can see, just who you are.

'Who are you?'

'I'm a man, come here, like lots of the rest.'

'I can see you have a fever in you.'

'Yeah.'

'I've got something to show you.'

'Show me then.'

(And he unfolds the door in the valley)

29.

Spin with me, under the valley, where we still think. And we still drink, the oil.

Spin with me, under the yolk of the dew of the morn, before the horn is blown and we are scattered under the radiance of his smile.

Hide with me, before we're found out.

 Before it's born.

Its hour come round, like a beauteous round, slouching his way, cutting a swatch through the dew and the corn, come round at last, O beauteous round, at the last, minute, instant, second and chance, avenue and romance, before everything, come round at shout, at Jerusalem born, burdened in your frequent burials of facts and older kings, we renew thee, you rough beast, seasoned and chanting, our rough beast, come round at last, under the valley, you rough beast, come round at last, O you rough beast, come round at last, at the last frame, the last luscious frame, come round at last, you rough Jerusalem, come round at last, come round at last, to the bedside, my child, do you see?

Buried in our seasoned regret?

Hungering in our toweled retirement?

By the pool?

Do you see in our despair?

His face, peeking out of the womb?

What rough beast, insisting, on his right, framed in the window, holding the leather over his feet, over his rough feet, burying the years in his eyes, what rough beast, his hours and hours and hours coming round and round and round, at last and at last, come round to Jerusalem, my son, to our terrifying pretend Jerusalem in the valley of Sunsborne to see its birth,

Hallelujah.

We carry the king on our back.

I carry the king on my back.

My hour is here.

My hour is come.

Only another midnight's child

to be born

send out the root
to my soul
and on the go the sinister to-fro of more and more
and more
just right
let out and say:

'well here you are. have you come to stay?'

hear me, in the foyer, blind on boots,

beating his heart heartily rue; tell me, do you want it?

'I know want to know what you know. Is it so bad?'

tell me; is it you burning, burning like a shelf, on my back, this train running nonstop into your frame, a self for fake and bake, lock warming and stun, my money and your thrumming whole, take me, and I'll take you too, to my home. Inside my ear.

Is it too far away?

'I don't know. Where is your ear?'

I don't know either. It moves around. The things it hears.

Watchword in the dark, my hearing to your ear. Will it betray you, do you think?

'you know better than me. But still, I want to know: where have you been?'

better betray me quicker, so I might love you. Love you better in the dark, where I am going. Going to betray me. Better in the midnight oil and sun. Better in the dark.

Betray me better in the dark, so I might know my own hearing, and so I might betray better too, to my truer you, on my long breaking midnight

heart. Tell me to you and I will mend, on the frequency which you mend dear, close to me and hearing. Hear me hear you in the midnight dark and I will be your friend, for as long as it takes, to make your wine and stink inside the dark, inside
'No betrayal is bitter. It is so many things. Like a love affair.'

You asked where I had been; it is only inside. You've been there too.

30.

My fire will stay you; put it out. Put it out in the dark. My dream is staying; I've seen it. Catch it in your hands. It wants to drift with us.

'This dream, have you had it before'

Many times. But not often with you. How about you? Have you dreamt with me before?

'I can't say. You seem familiar. Like a lover. Have we been lovers?'

Something like that. Perhaps even so; I don't know. I don't believe I can do it alone, though. I summoned you here, perhaps. Like a god.

'Ha ha ha all right then. I will be your god. Worship me.'

I do. And you are my tool.

31.

Let me tell you how it was, in the dream. And by dream, I mean reality. In the real I dreamt of.

I was dancing an Appalachian jig.

Because the world needed me. It no longer does, but in the truth of the dream I was needed. Because I could dance. Move my legs around on the porch. Stamp and hum my lips.

It is ocean we dream of; but no more.

I leave America and all its trimmings trummings truth behind me in a smokestack in a billgreen in a Brill Cream bullstream bullshit scene empowering paring pulling mass agony and waste I leave it; now.

It is ocean we are becoming; also, a waste. Like love.

These things don't mean what they seem. Meaning is a seeming, of course. We mean as we seem. AS though it could mean what we wanted. AS though desires had anything to do with meaning; they do not.

They are only ordinal coordinates; mapping the horizon.

Suggesting routes.

Planning trajectories.

Couching the delay, of the time to the match and the flame.

Alight with me, sailor, for I am the kingdom of night.

Here by my balustrade I break the night, in my corridor. In my rent ruin of my mind, streaming behind me in glowing threads of matter.

Here by me you are safe; I promise; for as long as I am alive in this dream you will be safe, no matter what else I say. And keep your own counsel too, of course. I'll need it.

It soothes me to know you come too; at sent shallow horizon with speed, loose and forward the bow, over the breaking waves of sky. Soothe me and know I wanted it too, after the end, and before we launched, but it's no matter. We are bonded by light.

'You say it's light? You're hallucinating. You kill the light, with your histrionics.'

Hahaha yes, have it your way, I am a fishwife, come thee and cut me, for my ruinous face is the ocean too, bent to bury you by its seaside. Cut me and ruin your face in turn, for the turning of the urn to you, by my burial side, by my ruin. Come by my ruin and know me, in my gleeful ruin, in my gleeful rise from the mountain of scabbed bark and seeds apples dark glass and fire smoldering come greet me in your ruinous smile, where I am, beating against your heart.

'I still think I know you. Do I? You can tell me. I... I promise... I won't hurt you. I only want to know.'

We were lovers. But it is all right. We aren't any more. It was more masturbation than anything. The journey is where love is; that is why we were lovers. And now we are truer lovers, you see. For we have forgotten one another, yet we remain together, in this.

'What do you want?'

It's coming. I need you here. Will you stay?

'All right.'

32.
The Night

Warm memories stretch around the black lives of trees, mesmerizing my mind in the freedom of the expanse of the dark. AS though I could dream away all the years and melt into the dirt, and the mulch and the fire.

He is here, cooking.

A handsome man. Like my brother. Keeper of winter.

He looks at me and I feel a chill. I know how far I've come. How far still to go.

These journeys: what do they mean?

They mean closer than meanings, I know; they remember us, are dreaming us, and are demanding us, being thorough with us, to know what we are and how to get us again, and better, lovers too, the road.

The road is the lover.

The road is the lover in the dark. Changing me like a fluid of love, to tremble before me desire for it, and for itself, in changing shapes and winters lost, and found, tremble before me, for I need it so much, your darkness and dream, in your powerful frame, shumming over my mind like a robe, like a curse. Curse me, with your winter's mouth, and shine over me in the dark, so

I can be afraid, so I can remember your face like no other.

No, there are many others. I can't demand less. But the lie is necessary; to insist that it is this road. There are many women but only one of them is with you. There are many men and each of them is here.

Light me and through:

Carry me into the dark.

I bear flame.

I bear witness to the coming of the light morning.

I am a prisoner of this oligarchy, coming back, to claim prize and witness.

Hear me and shit in the dark.

- -

I hurry into the dark on a bier. No, it is a palanquin. No; it is a bier. A bier and palanquin. To be delivered and to be set afire.

The fire is necessary for nobles; it purges us of our divinity.

For every American king, we kill is reborn, like a Hindu god, demanding we sacrifice him again, and again, and again. I am him; for that is what gods are, only actors. Beings playing roles in the dark. Men and women in masks.

Masque with me, Marissa, and shinder me to the solemnless oak, holy and broke. Be with me on the oak for our burial at sky; each star winking with us into the eyes of the knives.

My man carries me; I am weak. And old; though my body is young.

Just another noble dreaming in the dark. What a hideous figure! What a tragic mistake; to dream this darkly without music.

Dream even darker then; for the music is the darkness, isn't it?

'It's what I've been saying; if only you would listen. It isn't as hard as you make it out to be.'

Tell me then. How can we make it darker?

'Come with me'

The hubris mesmerizes the fate of my balls; to hang ever lower. To droop in the spoil of madness. To awaken and know their meaning in the roanoke of poems, written hued and bruised, for the burning youth of words, stilted in the pyre of our thoughts.

Burn me and bury us both; we die together.

'Was it good for you?'

We have to go soon. Whatever this is, it is coming closer. I needed you here not for sex but to be my right hand.

'You're wrong, it was for the sex, but believe what you like. Will you eat with me?'

Yes.

'This bread is from my mother.'

33. Dawn

Whatever it was has gone away, along with the man. Perhaps he was right; that this was only a kind of homosexual hallucination. I know it wasn't but it could have been. If I don't want it to return.

And do I?

And what is 'it', Robin?

The thing in the distance. The mark on the path, by me.

Bury me or build break launch shout shield and sear the fire by your face; here round. Here round sin send and sooth the merry trail your bright delay the burial rite and own; cheer me my galaxy my own cheer me, I am bright too.

Cheer me in the long regard the pull and steer the should and wean, the break and burial tear, hear me, break me, shade and shadow me, by night:

These lights delay describe the hate mercurial intense and loving huge patient and bright obtuse the ruin and the scraped tooth ruthing our heard poem;

Our heard poem a disease a badge a bloody iron gob.

Lick my bloody iron gob for the right side and the raw deal; lick my bloody iron gob for the high rate and huge steal my plaid; for seconds; the fire is dimming.

'What was that Robin'

These gods; they're all around. I thought you'd left.

'I went to see if we were alone; the war is still going on.'

It doesn't matter; they won't find us.

'Are you all right?'

It's coming back; that thing. It wants to tell me something but I don't know if we should listen.

'You should get some sleep. We have traveling to do soon.'

You're right. Thank you. Sleep by me, will you?

'I will keep watch. Here, lie here. If you fear in the night, hold out your hand.'

Thank you. I am a child still, aren't I?

'We all are.'

34.

Each word describes the thing but they are and must be the wrong words. It must be how this god works; that each thing should delay its passage round its face. TO near it but not touch. And in the nearness, we see. Like stars at the edge of our vision.

Lingering stars overhead; my lover gone.

No wilderness describes the torn of my beauty; no shield may shield me from the night.

I go in it to foot and wheat, beat keep and leap, toss staff and sheep, my each and heath, keep going Robin; one two for you it's all right.

It's all right I do it. It's all right I rule rail risk

I run rail risk

Run rail risk

Run rail risk

Is it enough Robin? Are you safe?

All round the night.

Tell me: are you all right?

'I'm all right.'

Who is that voice?

'It's me. Shut up.'

What are you?

'I'm you motherfucker. Shut up and keep going. It's not as safe as you think.'

I hear you.

'I know you hear me! I am you! Keep moving!'

Yes sergeant. Heave ho and ruin me; rake rave and thrill me, with your ease. With you mighty ease you thrill me, on the long night I rave and ruin your ocean, and I will again, each time, each time I will do it, with my fist, and with my staff I will infuriate it, with my eyes, I will infuriate it, kept open, and held swallowing, maneuver and stew.

'You have forty kilometers to go.'

What are we, in Europe? Give it to me in miles, Sarge. Miles!

'Thirty as the crow flies. Get moving.'

Aye aye Sarge! Aye Aye! Never would I dream of deserting you, you trembly fat Funyun! You fuliginous turban! You burdensome burial ground.

'Nor I you soldier. Step lively now.'

One two three four who unleashes the dogs of war, bark bark. Bark bark. One two three four who unleashes the dogs of war, bark bark.

'It is I. I have declared it.'

One two three four who unleashes the dogs of war on my lash my face on my last pace the moon who lashes and leaves me who reads and sees me who sheaves my hurt the fullness of the earth bereave me who shields me sends me greets and curves me who beats me, who beats me. Who beats me.

'It is I. I am your master.'

Who beats me I am yours in the shadow light in the fend forgotten light it is I. I do declare it on my yester yard on my solemn face the fear flows full below me like a loving plain river run my hurt is done will you ever leave me?

'Jump soldier!'

Ayyyyyyyyyyyy!

'Stay with me!'

Ayyyyyyyyyy!

'Stay with me soldier.'

I am dead.

'We're all dead men soldier. Keep marching.'

I'm a dead man on the train. Got women on the brain. Got to keep on moving through. With my ocean view, from the train.

'Twenty miles solider.'

Sally went by train to meet the postman Jack got to get her back on track back on the train; who hear the one about Sally; who heard the one about Sally, in her mealy mouth and her long beauty, as she steps forward for the dance, heave ho

'Heave'

Heave my ho on the lemon mountain, heave my ho in the steed; heave my ho on the bright turn of the track, give me the breeze. American breeze.

'We're American no more, soldier. You know that.'

Give me the American breeze, so I can hold my coat, step in to joke from the fog and smoke, give me a holler so we can be friends, on the East End and West Side, by the time I dry my eyes we'll be done, in the basement done, dead and done and shipped out, sorry for the sent away alarming gun, old friend, it's war, meant to be pure and right, like sunshine. Like a dead frisbee. Like a nuclear holocaust. Like lovers without number. Like love. War is love, Sarge, and I can hold my weapon short and stout, with my trousers in or out, and with my message writ into my gun, a romance lingering and full of doubt, gray and turbaned streets, or Rome, and the thrumming ocean all around, is it ho, say?

'Ho.'

Ho me and by the forge the fire; ho me and by the forge the fire. Ho me and by the forge the fire on the street my tan the coat; give me; keep me; hear my head sweep the street, on the limning grumpy bout, to the turn, oh give the turn to the long giveout in the sweeping cur to the cloudless south; give me the long get out to the musical wrath and the pouring count, to the end of the starry day. Give me the count to the end of the starry day and I'll press my face and shout, it's one two three till we get out, of this war--

'Love me. Love me if you can; I'm going over the edge.'

35.

betrothal is a ship of state sent merrily into the deep

creeping listlessly without its friends or weather reports

without reason or neglect

without legions or servants

without hue

the dew decks the storm

by our fireside.

patience brings slow reams of rewards in the dark

like fire in her eyes.

like tinkers in the storm

bringing burial masks to our scappered scrapes and skates over the surface of the ship.

betrothal is a mask we wear against the light

to keep the spite at bay and navigate the tremorous lesion of the spike of the world, hindered fast and straight, murderous.

nip and duck with me, under the branches of the sheltered vastness of the wood, under the sky, bear in with me to the future nearing, nearing, to port, nearing to port the bow and cue, rigid and struck phantomed black and bruised, the wood curled and mewling with a voice out of deeper caves;

break through

break through imbue the door with your abuse and cue the storks or wasps or muses for the cursing

curse well and loud

curse everything

stink right and through, the ship the world.

stink right and true, my boat for you

love

37.

Now I know the true reason; it exists, inside of my ears, underneath my brow. Here by my elbows, and screeching outside of the window, pain, fought low and held well, in the dripped bitter earth, lucky and meditative, like a shawl, over the old woman, divining the spirit of Man; her heart bids us to bow, before the great spirit, and know the world.

Her pain held tightly like a handful of grain for the winter march, after the last ocean, before the last rise, to the gull of the spoke in the shaft of the hills, trembling; my voice exists too, somewhere under my foot, for the gallery treasure, for the last minute before the last second of day, hearing the things that bring us closer, like love, or stars, stars, which are desire, de sidere, de sidere, de sidere, my love, and let the old woman sleep.

We, and we, and our weapons, hands, moving closer, in the minutes, and the hour, before we will endure again, the timing mass of the city each hundred villages clasping their weight to the air over our skin, their eyes and feet and generations tolling in their voices, horrifying bells, hold my hand, we are moving:

inside of the beacon of my voice

we are moving

to the center of this nodule of pain.

come into Sunsborne and shield your eyes from the light;

she startles you,

with the broad sunglass visage,

and the motorway over the earth,

over the trembling parlor divided equally into trembling parlors

carefully labeled

deserted

brightly painted

tremble before the regard of her majesty Sunsborne

in her alien eyes

we read the moments of our love.

come into Sunsborne and behold the weapons of Man:

our eyes

and our feet

and hundred machines.

but the chief machines are our eyes and our feet

moving over the landscape,

moving,

thinking,

feeling,

hopping,

designating targets and loam

deciding over factors incident in sunlight

in dream

in ocean and spite

in time for meetings and waiting, in walking

in walking.

in walking, our weapons invite us closer

to see it

this thing of us,

see us this thing,

overwhelming white lightning a thing without name

huge

vast

cyclopean

but with two eyes

Cyclops as twins,

As polyphemus had his brother

to smite the earth

to punish his mother

and her children

we tremble before God and one another

in the sultry pass of our delicious hubris and the scent of rain.

'is it true you killed a woman?'

'no, of course not.'

'but you look like you could.

'it depends which woman. Would you do it?'

'No.'

'Why not?'

'I'm not that kind of person.'

'Give it time. We learn here how we are when no one is watching. When the growth of destiny invites us to greed and weapons.'

'you're insane.'

'no more than most. have a drink?'

'all right.'

'I like that you're so close to me. I can smell you. A fever in you. It's so delicious. I want to taste you.'

'Do it then.'

when the city fades away,

leaving only the people.

38.

Betrothal is a weapon like doves, over the sky in the heat, shaking their winter coats, and knowing all they see.

All leave us behind; the others obey orders.

Angela watches the sky for rain, or disorder, and I watch her.

'we should go.'

'I haven't finished yet' she says.

'finished what?'

'this symphony.'

'you're high again.'

'so what?'

' so, it's getting on my nerves. we have to go. everyone's left.'

'there's plenty to eat. what's your hurry? Are you afraid of me?'

'Of course, I am. You're a woman.'

'Hahahah'

My arm around her shoulders shields me more than her; does she know that? Do women know everything? At least, about bodies?

These bodies of Sunsborne like parliamentary guards, stucco sentinels against a great and ghastly wind which seems unlikely to come but which they are prepared for despite all things. Despite all that could be.

Betrothal is a weapon of the senses, bringing things too close, making them blurry, making them shimmer in the light, making you weighty in knowingness, making you fire poured slow into your body, making the sky complicit in your moods, making the city own you, bereft of all sense, the senses surround your being with urgent victories, mysterious powers from distant horizons, secrets and passwords and messages rushing between you and the world. Betrothal is murder of the mind, shaking the heart and lungs into your feet and then out into the dirt so you can expire as quickly as possible, so these things will know you, at last, to know a thing, so desperate-- it is so desperate to know a thing, why would you do this--know a thing? And how?--its menace massacres the mind and strengthens the body, gluing you like cement to the world beneath your feet, to know a thing puts you in the dignitary's chair, at the cannibal feast. Which shall be your first meal, senor? Which organ of your body will be the food of god?

She is running over the asphalt.

TO be truth is the light, weaponized, sharp as the mind, cutting the stuff of the earth. I leer victorious with my sword, who is light, for my victory, who is all things, this series of moments of short life.

Truth is larger than betrothal but they are betrothed. Like a harem girl to her patriarch. Like leaves to a branch.

We simper in the sunlight to stretch our edgers into commiseration and obeisance to the stuff of the cosmos, wearing her contours like a sun her planets, my woman will never know me, as the moon will never know Earth, she shrinks slowly away from me each year, in digits perceptible to telescope and to my fingers.

This branch of the tree nourishes us in our pain, so we will know we are trusted and birthed. We are the weapons of god, which is only to say this branch, still on the tree, and wavering in the wind, knowing we can die at any time, to give ourselves this freedom to exist.

I am a tree in the sun for I am a being without name or victory, and I will remember you long after you are gone; the things come to me in the waves of light so I can be forgotten with them, and in passing, figure their name in the dream of my sleep, in the dark.

Dream of my sleep in the dark with me, and I will tremble before your touch, leaf by hand, wind or starlight, my moon blesses the countenance of your body so I will know who you have become and are becoming with me.

Betrothal is a mass whose quantity can be determined through sound, a bat on wing to the canyon. Sound with me

Screeeeeee

Screeeee

To summon the destination writ in the land, and I will define for you the limits of your world:

Each centimeter cut into your mind

Each passing of the sun ruinous to your peace in passionate rage.

'He's coming,' she says, and I smile.

There is still an ice cream man in town.

39.

War is coming. But what does it mean?

40.

Lilt low, sweet Henrietta, so I can hear your words, when you are enlarged in my mind.

Lilt low so we may remember your voice and the message it carries, of the road.

tell us of the road before roads, the track in the world.

tell us who knows your work here, and the work before, who works for you, and for yours, who makes you fear this world, and who will know your death, here?

tell us what words are yours, and which squints, which hurries and which pants, in the noon and the scurry before the coming government?

tell us who makes the world and who shuts it, who shants and who stints on the low green, who greets the morning with a smile and who with a whimper, is it you?

Which you is it that comes to the morning with your bustle and your bare neck?

Which you is it we must bury should you die, in the clasp of your weight, murdered within, by your own sheer stubbornness?

Which gasp in the moonlight is yours, bent burning and bewildered, in the stones of our fate, tell us, so we may be healed by thee.

Whose passion is it that you mar in the dust and in your bent carol, courteous and alone?

Whose rite curls in your lip, and in your steps, shifting our weight, under your boots, to bury us too, in your smiles and caresses, hideous and overwhelming, dust.

Whose history is it you write, woman in your piteous delights? Whose dances and whose visages of stone and mighty winds, cut canyons and regrets? Tell us the news you bring, in your raucous fell desires, in your movements of silk and your laugh careless divine?

Tell us the weight of your history so we can note it down in the years.

We feel our failure in your arrival; that we should not have known of it sooner, that what has happened to you--and we will never know it--came to you thus, and now to us.

Bad news is contagious but your deliverance is worse, and we crave it, for your piteous dignity is a sweet plague, cleansing us of madness and revivifying the world within our breasts, so that we remember we can speak, and know things we still know, and journey to the capitals of the world.

Henrietta lilt low and speak to us forever, binding us to the tirade of your eyes, and we are yours, in a moment and never spoken, never deviated, frozen and motionless, tired and bereft, holy, moving to the destination you name.

'Are you there, soldier?'

'Are you?'

'Is it you I see?'

'I'm right here'

41.

Yes, I rise to tell the truth; again, though it will be a weapon against me in future wars. Though neither of us is ready for it.

Every bus stop and every supermarket, every luminous morning, growing hotter, on every tar roof, subtle music.

42.

War is not yet come.

We're waiting; and there is freedom. Infinite summer worlds. The ream of women and men, planets, infinities, stretching round your arms, eyes, neck, hands, feet, over your head, under your belly, inside you.

The violence has subsided. The golden silence is terrifying but healing; the draft of the wind and the night and the peace who came before you were a boy, before anything else, it comes again, a regent in the kingdom of stars, just on a visit, in darkness and headlights.

Come inside and wait; the sun is down and the victory is closer, but don't think of it, we are together. There is nothing outside.

War is not yet come. I was lying. I am only dreaming it, like a dowager dreams of it, on her deathbed, thinking of all that is yet to do; all she might do in her diminishing power, all that is yet to come for her, she dreams.

It signifies the death of the soul and the birth of new entities, not souls perhaps but better, some reagent or fluid, postulate or mad theorem, Europa or Zeus, it doesn't matter, it's alive, I made it, it comes for me like a demon and I embrace its every curve, caressing it shamelessly in the fluorescent lights of my apartment, while the music plays and the city waits out its death, mercurial and delicious, oblivious cruel and monstrous in devotion to its penalties.

All my nights of my city forefend with me the diminution of meaning in this transition to whatever it is, we shall mean still, across the boundary; it is preserved. This is what meaning is. A signal boost.

Listen with me to the violin.

Its horror describes reasons we can still remember, in regions of the imagination we are not allowed to name. Its thundering visage is our own.

43.

pull me down into the night
disregard the day, it is not here but I am.

inside the window of the city storms carry the winter
carry the residue of affection
and bewilderment
over my skin.

pull me through the water to divines
or simply to some place I've never seen.
Let me dream.

I am drowning in you. I saw you somewhere; where was it? Not in a dream but in a city, I have never seen. The rigid walks of monarchs and the glee of burning townships strip me in your presence shift me in your presence stilt me and make me wait for deliverance.

Deliver me from you so I can wait; again, for you.

I owe you. This winter's guest. The liquid night and strong ocean. The scent of time.

There is no reason; no substitute. There is no excuse; no escape. From the truth.

No, fear me, I come raging and foaming, fearful and mad, scraping my metal arms against the

pavements and smashing all the windows I see .
. .

- -

Sink me, and clutch the night tight to your chest, as she moves over you, in her infinite frequencies, in her promises and spitefulness, the spirit of the city come slow and fine, who is her name?

Whose paths and purchases plucked passionate and painterly from your head, rigged rolled and rugged into the trunk:

The door to revolution lies upstairs in the attic (bats in the belfry), up in the space between the roof and stars.

Behold the season of regret and loneliness, O mind controller, behold the long goodbye and nectared neck of the regal mask, sent to and forward to the doom room, sly fly and curled, spending her spendthrifts on the plastic floor;

curl me, and catch all catcalls all weights and wisps of air measurements and symbols havocal bright wet and red; murderous serene, my friend:

Sink me into this night and be prepared to be your own version of your enemy, like a good CIA agent, sunk into the clone-wear, breathing the same air, believing in the melody of thought like scholars in the words writ onto the page; cluck cluck my favored puck we hearsay:

we hearsay and hear say the heard shears of the ear police, kept closer now and still; roar out over the sky.

Roar out over the sky.

Roar out over the sky ebony rich wrinkled messenger mass wavelength mix and mull the word the world mess right and rim roll down and dim the earth the hurtling turn and curl of the divorce from the stars and from the burling haystacks below;

We fly.

Mental executioner! Priestly scholar! Reader of tragedies! Poet and philosopher! Old woman! Old woman; fly.

These are our serpents and our hindered beasts; our shadow treats and sterling savages wrinkled and neat, the palpy wrecks and stern statuettes of lingering empire, writ into our skin, our eyes.

Behold the enemy ourselves, in our flying power, in our long divorce, from the real:

Behold our power, over everything.

Like gods.

Our songs of ourselves; worlds infinite.

Sing me this song of myself, and I will show you something different, from the earth spinning before you, or the Black Mass dancing behind you, I will show you fear writ into the space between thought and dream; nurturing you, keeping you wet, weighty, and bemusked to the task of making our kingdom grow;

Old woman; grow this kingdom queendom will you, lady?

Old woman! This song of yourself so beautiful. How can I hinder it?

How can I insist on these limits?

Limit the truth?

Under the lemon lights the ruin of my city greets me, delicious, loud and calm, murderous and patient, this love affair, bright and bilious forward broken moving, moving, moving:

heal me in your midnight, your inner ruin, in the blocks and stones. In the dank dust and dirty melancholy rooms the rich bath and waste the mash the fate and looms spun in the shadow house inside the hill grow slow and out heal me in the black midnight and blood in the mess and mirror of your thriving stare in your colony of sharpest words, your network of new life ... this house

thrill me in the noondark; where I am swimming, where I will wait, for you:

44.

I begin again, and it is mine.

All legions and fields.

These men; built back and new.

War;

(war)

War.

In this sidereal display of the servant to his court, we'll receive orders:

like a symphony, cut to stand, dwelling over the falling bits like a reluctant coyote, our dreams stuffed into our mouths, our leering visage cut open, we are celebrated in the light.

Celebrate with me.

These dreams are open to us; it is no small opinion.

The conflux of the raft and the reed, made haft and heeded by our arm, our weight, our memory, on no river--not even reality--but a storm.

The storm of reality cut maximum rich dwelling splashing our face, insulting our family, luxuriating in our despair, and spinning monstrous labyrinths round about us, plumbed in the depths of our souls, each maze figures the maze-goer, in his despair and triumph, the fading view of the sky, and his world, kept to forbearance and keeping our souls straight, as a meteor, as an oven, huge, diaphonic, languorous and new, our triumph satiates the will with its miasma, it cuts the lungs out of their head, it writes the name of the holy vestments of women over our eyes, blackening us, barraging us, damning us to our knees, pushing us down.

Push me down and bear with me the silent night before the next storm. Like a terminal illness, reality will not let go. It does not lessen. It increases; it does not subside. It will not turn away. It will not lesson or move or shift, except towards us, its center prizes us from our minds and flings us around its body, spiral messengers without will.

I begin again; is it mine?

Whose is it?

Whose name and whose dress?

All who thought here too are dead; but their dying is sweet on my tongue. I can taste the dead. Like a rich fluid. Like honey.

I dream of the dead in my speech; I work their bones and chew their gristle; I move their mouths to make my words.

Who approaches in the night?

'I will give you a gift.'

Go away. I don't want it.

'Memory. You will remember.'

45.

Set to reverse around the orb of you, bounty hunter, big dick bailiwick centurion cosmonaut nailrunner spitemonger; O Astronaut Song of Myself; quell the engines and let breathe the Roman guillotine (a star);

Gnosticism still insists the reasons have a meaning, determinable in the ephemera of interactions between you and the world — more; a message.

The medium is the message but this means signal is noise; each category of understanding turbulent as a woman; bent to scrubbing a floor.

Scrub the floor with me and make music; each glance from the sky from the door each broken branch in the hall each memory eclipsed by the present, determined by the present, and vice versa, stemming a chord, holding the violin:

Here the reader meditates on a poem.

Bend the light;

Break the verse;

Undo the obverse side of the sun;

Rip down the scaffolding and the mud;

Run the gamut of the dialogue between Man and God;

Ruin the Earth;

Ruin my Earth I am already a Ruin;

Rape me;

Round my house.

Thrill my doubt and fill my oven with your memories;

I burn.

I am burning everything.

Bend tighter than the sun and elicit the wavelength of thought;

Accrue the interest on the debt!

What, have you not paid?

Let us bring out the accounts!

Let us divorce the debt from the tinder house!

Let us reason the meaning of a song!

Let us disguise the universe in a poem!

Let us greed.

Let our greed fill the city!

Make shift and dance on the umber poems, waiting for the sky;

Eclipse the drift and see;

My healing bliss;

In our careful tryst betwixt sand and waves.

Have you bent so to get the meaning from poems?

Here in the starch right. Here in the emblem and glance. In the hot night.

Shift dance and weight the bands ring out the stands on the evernight, ring out the stands on the evernight and greet my holidays advance, greet my holidays advance over the moon; over the dark.

Curve the words into the dark; I cannot hear you.

46.

Sunsborne and its districts; a poem.

Written in fever.

Where we turn on the bright lights.

Turn on all the bright lights.

Turn on the bright lights, girl.
"Like this, Daddy?"
Yeah, like that.
"What is it?"
What's it look like?
"It looks like stars."
And what are they?
"Little suns!"
Big suns far away.
"How far away?"
Real far away.
"How can we get there?"

We're already there.

47.

Thrill the rung of the stomach gung, lightning and thunder by the trance of the summer break and stumble; by the last night.

This night is careful went and klept serious foredone, a rock and a neighbor, a Jungle Gym.

Orthopedic marks on the estuary of night; the sound of the clouds.

Turn on the bright lights and bear the weight of the universe; it doesn't weigh much.

Turn on the sun and bring the clasp of the coat of the wooly scarf over your neck; over your future.

Here lie the days of the Earth and the reach of the mercury; here lie the links of the dove and the stems of the serpent's teeth; stilted onerous savage beautiful wings.

Stilt your savage beautiful wings and stay a while in the humble dress of a poem; stark the fluid of your dream with the wash of poetry, white over the grey; stem the leaving of your body in the writing of a mass for the body of stars, humdrum and liquid.

48.

We're killing.

Killing everyone.

But what reign do I intend?

Are you my friend?

Is it so with you?

Have you reckoned much with the meaning of poems?

49.

Beat the barry and the hearse, set the home into reverse and set the frame afire, set the bury on the munster son and glow the weapon to her face, make the mace her heart.

Each nobleman deserves a poem, written by the wise.

Set her face her eyes and set your knife.

Make music from your poem and lull the stew of the day, mule the verse of the storm out of your thought.

Kill the noble and rule as you are taught; glorious.

Rent the rack and coil the ruse, muse the furnace and the hearse.

Stack the belly and assert the truth; shake the firmament.

Glue the words and grasp the earth; beauty is a curse but it is born in you, like lightning, like a river of lightning, ungluing the masses of men from their work to the fight.

Unglue in you and start to; this is my epitaph of who I was.

Commoner poetry, Whitman. You and Primo Levi, with your chemical leaves.

50.

Cut the belly and raise the bends.

Burn the hostel and the waiting friends.

Bury the body and deliver the news; it's raining money.

Raining money on the day of the revolution.

What shall we buy with thee?

You're money, honey.

You're the sweetest money I've ever seen.

Cull the crowd and set the tune — it's here for you to use — it's religion and it's obtuse, but there is no better blunt force trauma.

Her shawl is a sepulcher for your history, cleave to it as to her back in bed, the word is a world but it delivers you; you must kneel;

Kneel under the weight of the frequency; it passes over you like an F-16, but you can see it, for the moment, of the passing, its gravity and thunder, its geometry and its wings.

Each word is an F-16; more powerful than; and my war is religious.

51.

Religious war is a nighttime war; fought with knives.

Here, see my knife.

52.
It's sharp, isn't it?

53.

See here a nobleman sleeps. Beside his wife.

Under their chardonnay.

By the bay.

Outside the ducks.

Inside his heart, just another man.

Keeping his peace by the ocean.

Set his house aflame and keep his head over your hearth, as your ancestors did.

The head is a weapon too.

Like a word, it sets the world to it, reaching for fog where it finds delight, and making the world into its weapon, sighting its ears to the long divorce of sound from fluid, metal from onions, lover to lover.

Set the word to its divorce and murder the family from its home; mail the loot to your mother too. You little Viking.

Vike with me and still the night; let me entertain you.

I am yours.

I am your minstrel and I will whisper in your ear, of Votan and his many kings, thundering under his hood.

Vike by me the metal and the mirror, the murder and the weal; vike with me the cloudy fluid of blood and the lovely tenor of dawn, vike with me the princes and the kings of the world.

I may not be American but I do like killing kings.

54.

Is there anything sweeter?

55.

Black the light and bury the name; bleed the burial and make the music; mark the movement of the stars over your face.

All religious war informs the movement of the sea; meets the marriage of the deep to the skull; melts the liquid in your thumb; in your heart.

All religious war informs the source; kept to port and wondering for the captain: does he live? Does he remember? Each course is starry but it's to a purpose;

Yes, bury my heart at wounded knee but then dig it up again.

For my zombie heart, will not die.

56.

Bell the burial hymn; break the shower over her head; bless the union of thought to remorse; the marriage of skull to ape.

Bless the union of black to white, and day to dark; heartache to divorce; bless the union of the marriage to the deep, whose voice sounds nightly in my sleep.

Bless the union of the starry kingdom to the sea of the sky; and bless its rivulets of time searing over my shoulder, pearl in my palm.

Bless the union of muse to writer, whose kisses tickle my fingertips.

Bless the union of curve to weight; shift to shroud; shell to lizard and mark to meaning; bless the union of the pen to the pull of the mask of the curve of your curse to the firelight weight of your revenge; she shrieks it too; our lovers in their nightly rhythms our children in their delight;

Bless the union of the star to the deep, and its quenching; bless the union of the lingering pause to the poem; to Pinter; to Pindar; to Plato.

Bless the union of purple to blood.

All purple will die.

57.

Kill me purple on the spot; at once.

Kill me purple for a long feast.

Kill me purple for a wintering night and a winter kingdom. Kill me rain for the limpid pause and the soft retreat, from the starling midnight sun.

Kingdoms and stars have a lot in common though it's unscientific to think so . . .

58.

Die with me and live again; it doesn't hurt too bad.

Die with me and live again; it's a delight.

Die with me and shriek the names of the damned; it's yours.

Die with me laughing; with your knife in your hand.

Cut my hand and I'll bleed for you.

Each night the devil waits, for my word.

59.

Attend with me the devil and prepare the rites; for his words are true.

The devil is a good man; I know him. He fights for us.

Listen.

60.
A burial at sea

61.

Hold my hands and wait. Pass out from society! Haha!

Heal slow.

Explore the ream and the whirl; expiate your sins in the violence of your launch, from orbit:

62.

Writing is a priesthood and I worship my god, reality

63.

I worship thee.

In your blunt stock trauma.

In your bleeding midnight.

In your gun-in-the-mouth truths.

Your boiling oceans and brittle staves of weight, kept hurried and worn beneath the stoves of our feet:

64.

Gloomy glow and roomy ruin! Heal the stars and whet the wickets! Whet the ruin and the rinse from your hair of the grease of the pale fluid of dreams.

Share the shield and steer the hearse into the bier;

Light it up baby.

Light it up baby and storm the house, shake the steel and murder the copse and case.

Fire me;

Fire me now.

65.

Fire me and fire me now!

66.

Set to, and on fire, in the soul door, come here.

Come here.

The days spill over the mountain, heeding our request for healing.

Hurting in the night.

Hurt in the night with me, under the penalty of the daylight, to break passage to tomorrow.

Or even to noon.

Break through to noon for me, and wield the hour, scribbling facts and figures, noting the alignment of your face

to hers, and his, the change in the weather, the shape of the field.

The field is shaped like you: run and burnt, low and smoky, grasping at the sky.

\- -

The weapon of time sits on the windowsill cooling, mesmerizing the cats and the clouds.

Storm this daylight for a sound, shake this town for the river, and come on down:

Prescience holds in your elbows and back, to determine the course of your eye:

Next to thought is being, negotiating, thrilling the earth with its syncopated harmony, gluing the raft to the weft of the water, hurling its hair round its head:

The weapon of time sits in your lap, firing the deep.

Wield it.

Everything which you suspect designed to subject you to pain is just so; that is its purpose.

We will burn the torture chamber as soon as we locate it; it is all around us.

67.

Bear in to the duff under your feet an ache willful word of your power in afternoons; scuffling your toe into the crusty bark of the forest, leavening spread over the weeks and months of the fires of California;

Inside a dream the maelstrom describes a beginning; begin now

begin now;

begin now;

68.

I am a keeper and this is my village, in Sunsborne. I keep thee, on my mountain axe, and my fire sea, on my live-a-day iron-key straight hut born south burn right born for me, kept Saturday and midnight, I keep thee, on my mountain axe over the myth, the fuel and the settling into the armchair, into sleep.

We are Sunsborne.

And our many districts are one.

Swim, in the searing black water, herd your feints and fears into your bowl, of your tummy. Load aloft your eyes and hair, your back and bowels over the surface of the black water.

Bear the burden of your tome; hideous alive.

Hideous and hideous alive.

A disease.

A friend.

A package, for delivery.

Bear the burial of your youth on the waves like so many cousins before us; bear into the black water.

Bear with me to the east, to the land,

On our backs,

Into the dark.

Sunsborne has no limits.

We are a nation like Jews: bound by story.

Shout with me into the storm.

Open your mouth, and shout.

Shout with me.

Shout with me.

69.

I AM AN AMERICAN BORN MAN LIKE WALT WHITMAN A LONELY MAN AND POOR I WRITE POETRY ON A MACINTOSH LAPTOP THAT RUNS WINDOWS 7 I LONG FOR THE DEATH OF BILL GATES AND JEFF BEZOS AND NEW YORK CITY I AM THIRTY-SIX YEARS OLD AT THIS WRITING THIRTY-SEVEN IN SIX DAYS.

I AM LISTENING TO THE NEW YORK BAND BY THE NAME OF INTERPOL.

INTERPOL IS US PARADING AROUND. ARE YOU REAL? HAVE YOU STRUGGLED HARD TO LOOK INTO THE MEANING OF POEMS?

NOT HARD ENOUGH. I GUARANTEE IT.

STALWART BREAK MY BACK ON THE BAILIWICK MOTHERFUCKER, BREAK MY BACK ON YOUR OLD BOARDS AND I'LL SCREAM.

GO AHEAD:

TAUNT ME AS LONG AS YOU WANT.

I AM NO LONGER AN AMERICAN IN MY HEART.

AND WE ARE ARMING OURSELVES TO OVERTHROW NEW YORK AND WASHINGTON AND SACRAMENTO AND ALL OUR CAPITALS.

WE WILL DRIVE THEM FROM THE CONTINENT.

70.

Scream with me into the black water; we sail east on the movement of our hate.

Every storm meets a sea, her passage is victory, over the evening midnight poem.

Hear me, clasp the sea, on my terrible midnight berth, in my birth wiggling dire and straight, black as the ball of burning;

Parade me over the fire and I will keep thee in the movement;

In the movement and the parade.

Parade with me over the midnight fire,

And I will dream with thee of your own dark,

Hurting too;

Like onions,

Like time,

Pine trees.

Cleave to me and I will swim,

I hear the children crying to us, over the dark water,

By the land.

Bury me by the land and I will grow a tree,

Threatening the sky.

71.

We know the rivers run, explicit.

Time corridors or dreams in the water, here on the island.

We know the river is spirit, naming names.

Each thousand thousand of them.

Time is a river too, lapsed for the midnight hours of our arrival.

In the dark, see the curling water and let it heal your stories, patiently devolve your prejudices into wordless cries, straighten your forelocks and your divines, making music from your body.

Music in your body remembers the reasons better than you do.

Deliver me into the poem in my dreadlocked block dark ruinous boots stomping the ground deliver me into the sea of grass.

Deliver

Deliver me into the sea of grass

I am your burial ground.

Your last wave

Your first kiss

In the eglantine sea of grass

72.

Bear me and bear within, the temple den of your heart.

Kept my dark divine over your night sky, ruinous and holy; shanting the thoughts over your cape.

Cold my approach to your dark;

Kill my thought to heart in your embrace.

Shift me

Soil me

Stare me trample me and deliver me

I am mill man to your marry hand;

Hurry me back west.

Hurry me back west to the war.

73.

War is beautiful.

Like a woman is beautiful.

74.

Curve the fire and mark the waste, save the trail and wear the rest over your shoulder, like a monument to departed countries, heal the vale and spark the trace, of the ever afternoons marching in place beside your feet, on the street, hereafter and now, both, written into your bones.

British means "tattooed," and so my blood is one of marks, these old gang signs.

Gang sign with me, and wield the wending arc of allegiance, to so many things. So many allies, crawling out of their buckets, and dropping from the sky.

Sloughing their skins and their weird regards, for the masque, of the play.

Play with us by the sea, and see our jumps, five hundred meters, elastic phantasms, bodies moving in the noon, rich and free.

Well, Angela doesn't like it.

'What are we doing, hmm.'

Preparing.

'For what.'

For war.

'I've had enough. I can't take this shit anymore.'

75.

Lemon traces in the salad. Meteors overhead. The night is alive with music. Hear me, in the aftertrace of the neon godhead, quantum ephemera coursing over your skin in British inflorescences, nubile and vast, a tract of space undulating on wax, hurtling over our embrace, of love.

I am a man; but what does it mean?

76.

My woman is gone. But my army remains.

This grave and terrible romance.

77.

Writing is god.

Let me sing to you.

78.

Hey in the mountain hey in the fever hey in the back in the dream. Hey in the morning hey in the afternoon; hey by the sea. Hey on the mountain hey in the fever; hey by your dream. By your leave messieurs by your dream messieurs by the ocean by your dream. By the ocean.

Send out, and send in, each method for the opening din; ribald and furious. Horrendous and mercurious; stupendous. Luxurious. My own note. On my own city. Sunny born and sunny sent, to the war:

79.

No; something has gone wrong.

I cannot describe it. Something in the water.

I must resist the overly simplistic so it is not an evil come over the land; this is not Tolkien. But something new.

This new dark thing worming in; small at first, but growing larger. Until I can't take it . . .

80.

Run poetry into the sun; be light.

Be sick to heal and ruin war; we can say; for a moment . . . say: it's all over.

We triumphed, as all things do. Now let us shut our doors.

Shake the cabinets. Explode the sinks. Tear through the roof, powder the windows into clouds; make the house dust and our family servants to the barren void:

Now we undertake the emolument of the breathtaking feat of desire: greed's gift to the world, in honest foreplay and murderous excitation:

The world, the win, and the ruin, this beauty:

What was it came over you?

Who were you with?

What room did you hear the words in?

What was it you did?

In the black mass before sunset and noon; pleading the gift before the president, and leaving too early.

Well, it's all right. We all had things to do.

We all had corpses to bury.

Wounds to patch up.

Traumas to hush in the night, when they return.

Turn with me, to the light, where I keep my steed;

He is trembling in the shade.

His eyes reveal the nature of this journey.

Get on, and speed into the turning of the wheel:

Part 2

81.

Pull out all the stops; the juice is loose, on my awl into the wood, on my oath.

No man shall see right; I have forgotten.

We have been arriving for some time. With our many tears. We are arriving now.

Over the ocean.

I want to tell you: I remember your face (even though I fear I have forgotten it) – in the laundry, in the onions, in the luggage, in my hat.

In the silence of my soul I meet strange rewards: the numinous volcano of the imperial distance – I measure it out by the league, determining the shape of morality.

In this silence, I slip my tongue under my teeth and down into a bowl:

I hunt spare change.

Give a beggar a chance on the long knife, the industrial silence of the street delivers my words swiftly: spare a little change for a strong brother.

Look in my bowl, in the milk: I nourish a dragon whose name is Lore.

Feed him if you like; he will live inside of you.

The work-ruler America stands over us, cracking the whip. His slaver's eyes so sad.

Come let us dance with him, leading him by the hand around the mountain, curving up, for the sacrifice:

At last, the slaver will be employed. We have given him a job, answering the telephone.

--

The sea lives inside me. I am on a train, heading north. The rails mark decisions, over the landscape; the cars sit, squat toads in the plain.

Now the sun shimmers over my face, healing me from past blessings, and reminding me of the dangers in play.

Swords, and witches. Kingdoms and friends. The ocean.

The sun is familiar with the ocean.

Sleeping over the waves.

--

Now all kingdoms recede. I am driving. My sheep. To market.

82.

run tight with me
I remember;
how you were;
how you held me, when I was young.

I am bright, bearded and breaking;

I am breaking;

over the sand

- -

take three, and take two
for when I'm right there over you
in my dreams

83.

Angela is away; inside the deserted discotheque. Some of the sausage-sellers have not yet left; I buy one from them, holding it tight in my hand under the palms.

I will watch her for a time, in my mind, feeling the physical distance between us; about three thousand yards.

Some of the deep things watch me too; echoes of the past. They are still here, of course, not really past, so much as half-forgotten. Memories of the ancestors: still fresh.

Now Whitman is dead; so, I sing for his funeral.

All hail Whitman!

We shall celebrate him forever.

He has died again. In Brooklyn.

I feel his beard on my cheek.

84.

Now we know America is destroyed and it is a great comfort to us; the dream breaks and we wake, scratching our heads, wondering what it is has happened.

All of the people are joyous in our despair; there is nothing so certain as an end.

We look at each other and nod, spent, wondering, a little, but mostly filled with a strange and dull contentment, of the coming deeds, but more, the simple feeling itself, of a new weight over the chest, smothering the mind, and lifting our eyes to the sun.

So, cheerful demons come, in their secrecy, to dance with our bodies.

Angela has left but she left me with the apartment and some people have started to return. I've been talking to one of the old poets in the walls and he tells me not to believe it, that the people are not real, but I know he is insane.

I have grown sane, it seems. What a strange thing. As though I had been poisoned by the truth and survived.

I am appointed ambassador to Sunsborne;

This is me.

A new city being born.

It is fun; I shouldn't admit it, but it is. To be given the duty of reporting bad news.

I grieve, for my city is destroyed, and I can say it with a smile.

85.

Now we are waiting and hiding, smiling into the heat. Our bad bodies nourishing the wind. We wait for the creeping cull under our weight, a train symphony under the metal and stone, under our tongue. If it should speak we might explode; so, we hum along with the train, to know that we are part of it, and it must not come out all at once.

I shake, the reducing valve attached to the steam drill, riddling my teeth with the music of redemption, as my bones are shattered, and my eyes bleed. It is joyous to be united with our machines, who heal us, and keep us alive, and watch us in our winters and in our sleep.

Almost I am a kind of machine too, waiting patiently for death. In my movements, I can deny myself the correct pleasures, and linger over the incorrect ones, musing at how my course has been shaped by so many men and women, who linger too, over me, muttering:

"What a bad egg."

I am a bad egg and it is my destiny to fight you and so I do; with the words of my mouth and the keys under my fingers, sparkling, to get you out; I will banish you; I will turn you from the Earth; I will know what you are.

What are you?

How many hens? And how many wax men?

How many blessings and how many turds?

Is it all right to say that we are arriving?

Well, I'll say it. Who cares if it's true; it might be.

We are arriving. I shall play music.

86.

Today is my birthday. I am thirty-seven.

They have given me a good perch; though also they threaten me, saying I will soon be thrown out.

The manager has pointed out that I am too tricky; but I think he suspects I am a kind of weakling.

Me, I don't know what I am or why I have been given this job.

But I enjoy doing it; I suppose that is why it was given to me. Like a bell knife, cut under the diaphragm, to hasten the breathing. Like water runs over the surface of the sky, glaring its eye out of my head.

What is the point of the destruction?

It cannot be to avoid it in future. And certainly, there is the simple pleasure in it.

Yes, it is the pleasure of its inevitability, but more, the character of it.

Each burning must go well and some brave ones will describe it, saying that it was this particular thing, now marked on maps, for us to know, in case it should become relevant.

I am relevant but I fear I may get too hot; the lever increases with each sound around my apartment. I don't want to lift the Earth; I only want to live in it.

87.

Now many things become clearer, though not clear enough. The terrible thing about revolutions is you can see, feel, as they are happening, the decisions your ancestors made in similar ones. The grave decisions they made so you wouldn't have to make them. Only now you do.

In revolutions, you think: well, what a pain in the ass. Nothing is as clear as it should have been. Some things were too true. Some annoying things kept coming back.

How quickly must I act to make the things true? The things that I want.

88.

Crash out with me; on the bed, in your chair, from the world; nap.

Crash beneath the district of our melancholy keeping measures, metal, oil, rubber, steel and mesh, threshing the works of our brains and our heads into mylar drumbeds coruscated between apartment buildings . . .

Crash out and rest.

89.

Gloomy midnight poems cheer the soul; my all for you though I am small.

All small, and all cheery, in my spite and in my leery loam, I grip you, in the slick suds of the earth;

Tell me; don't tell me;

I saw you. We are one; though I've forgotten.

Tell me the reason and I'll tell you the spite, in swift regard and after, turning luminous, linked gravities, hurting the rigid moon of my soul, arms blithe round its dripping trunk, the globe of a secret religion secreted beneath great trees:

Tell me it's over and I can forget, that all I've et is healthy and I'm no longer needed.

Tell me I'm no longer needed.

90.

Tell me how it'll go with me when I am set out on the table with the meat; when I dream of fishes over the sky. When you come too, sitting by the table I lie on, to await the right moment for the feast.

Tell me the treat of your regard as we walk; through the reeds.

Read to me in your voice; I'll listen. These roads extend within, behind the hills and burning lisps of centuries split over them we grin to make the rhyme extend into our mouths:

Tell me the reason and the sweat; tell me you bet on me and I'll regret the time I choked you to death, with my dreaming:

Tell me the ocean's wet and I can be surprised; tell me the saintly things we did were real and I can remember all the snatches from my sleep that still make sense on waking, how to fit them into my step, how to glue them to my brain.

Walk with me and make me fret; I need it; I saw you first.

91.

Send me a letter and I'll send it again I'll bend it in the light when I see how it delivers me; how it renders me in the corpus Americana bilious in the wind, deranged and somnolent, leering at the turnpike . . .

Send me the future and I'll hold on tight, whipping over the motorbikes and the streams effluent running over the dry earth . . . sail me higher.

Send me the sun and I'll rejoice; my place extends its arms into the silent skies and silent stalls around my fort; I see you up above.

I'm waving.

92.

"You're still here."

Angela stands by the door.

"Where else would I be?"

"Come outside with me," she says.

She's dreaming with her eyes; making tea in the street. You can still do it, although some traffic is returning. We sit close to the curb, staring down the avenue towards the pale blue buildings.

The cup in her hand circumdescribes us as though revolutions could be reduced to a computer's login session, devaluing its bliss in increments, awaiting the next command.

Holding melody and right, wordless righteous — untrue, perhaps, but good enough — plastic in time.

Groovy, man. And it does have a groove, cut into the porcelain. Tea and a woman and the reality smokestack, cut higher for the cue, now approaching...

Tend my ruin, would you, I need to wait for some deeper summer, one that knows my name. Still I am anonymous to it; how hot does it have to get before it knows my name?

Magnifying my hope, in my hand, green tea and red hopes, sailor, red sky at morning, fear me;

Fear me;

We drink the tea and stare at the rising city, now different, Sunsborne but some new district sans name, and my shoes, still eager to beat the asphalt, for absolutely no reason:

It's black tarmac on track to whack my theme, for I dream of a drowned mars city cut orbed and tethered to my trick, she slips beneath the rim of the moon-lit wave inside the drug, but I don't have time for that now, caught inside my own.

I'll pull a thousand poems round her ears, and mine too — if only it would mean the things I thought it would.

If only poems were bombs, and I could target them like the Pentagon.

Pentagonal processional at large, at heat, white heat, and white Mars, burnt to magma, smoking round the gun, of my typing fingers . . .

Shake my solemn energy at rounds, astounds, my ear to the ground listening for the reason of my birth.

This worth extends around my hands, and the weapon ultimately is simply that, I think, the gravity well of my hands, greater than any kinetic ghost of a coitus smoking military round spun rifled into the playground; the truth; or what's left of it; come round at last, in his evening garments, ready for a meal, and a toke, and a look at the sky.

"What time is it?" I ask her, and she smiles, because she knows what time is it.

Time for a farewell fuck and clean the room after; we're leaving town.

93.

Something without a name. Moving over the landscape with a woman. This thing with legs, called me, sworn to protect the boundaries of me, as well as to savage the boundaries of her, working to forget everything I can, so I can keep my eyes open and my mind engaged with the landscape before my eyes.

The wise man is right that time is only a useful fiction; it can exist or not, as it pleases. Right now, it is on vacation, and I am grateful for it, so I can remember certain things of the ancestors, behaviors and thoughts untranslatable into English, though I should try. It is why I write this book, after all.

Sinking the bucket into the well. And hauling up the trace elements, launched from a star, into my mouth.

Ruses of faint daylight reflected in my glasses soothe my soul and dip me down around the dust of our feet heading into chaparral, looking for the others.

There always are some.

Aren't there? Aren't you reading this?

This record is a lie but I need it; as I needed her then, and the dust and the sunlight. It summons my body to its needs, and it did then too.

My body needs memory, which it constructs as I write, so that it will know what it is, whose purpose it serves, and why.

A kind of averaging effect.

Though it may stone me in its brutality.

94.

Perhaps I resemble the state that is trying to destroy me; writers and states both demand obedience, both are dissatisfied, both lack humility and both are determined to succeed despite all odds. Both ascribe to themselves this kind of primacy over the world, the primacy of the ape, prime primate.

I would be a philosopher except then I would have to invent rules, and no story or poem I wrote would be free of them, because I would be doomed to polish and strengthen those fetters in everything I wrote. Still, I need it, for it gives me the distance philosophers depend on, sheltering me from the world.

95.

Fish on Friday. Mix on Saturday. Ocean on Sunday, by the pier. The feeling of empire, like a leaden weight, not unpleasant, settles over my shoulders and is resident in the air over the small crowd, watching waves, eating French fries, thrumming in quiet contemplation.

Angela no longer sleeps beside me but still fucks me; in obeisance to the righteousness of our bodies' needs, and contradistinct from the shoveling off of our collective warmth, readying for a warm California winter by freezing our hearts against any movement towards the other:

I am asleep still; I know. Waking is a kind of torment. I can only take brief snatches of it before settling back into the throng of the beast of the night (whether day or night), the night of sleep-while-awake, sleep within sleep, and the dozen half-asleeps so little measured, perhaps because immune to measurement.

I am alone; another reason I began this record, of course. Yet writing wakes me; forces me to remember who I have become.

It is all right, Robin; most will not care; some remember it too; others are offended and will not read anything you have written, so you are safe.

I am safe when I write. Like murderers are safe, only in the act of taking life.

I scratch my mark into the tree, and though I have seen no one for days, I know it will be seen, understood, and either obeyed, or not, as suits the reader. My mark says:

I have seen things. What a vision. We can't know what it is. But we understand that something has happened.

96.

Something is happening. Not here, not like the Buffalo Springfield song, it is not here that it happens, and also unlike the song, it is clearer now what it is. The song is appropriate, because it knows that revolution is an instant, but the song was bleary on the details, being ultimately a decidedly unsober revolution . . .

This one is sober, or more so. This one is brighter, like daylight brought out through a filter — or the filter removed — the radiation a tad more real, and more reliant on your own body.

This is what radiation is; it is a relationship; a system of connections between you and space.

Space says: there you are. And you say: well, if it isn't space.

Something happens in my body when I am writing this; like the other times but smaller, a beaujolais cluster of forgetful adjectives, strumming under my tongue, waiting for the whispered word of accord, an adjustment, to forefend with my mouth the coming lecture-hall motifs and snarls, the resentments and untoward abuses, the King, and his Castle, and the Many Residents within, now thundering their bad music in our wake, insisting still that it is okay to be a slave, please, come back, we didn't mean it, we shall lighten the load, you are needed, please slave, come back, I won't call you a slave anymore, you are a worker. Special worker in our kingdom; please come back.

The low volume of my intercourse with my subject is worrying; again, things have finally gotten serious. *Endlich es ist ernst* and I don't know what to do about it, can't know, I suppose, until it is already upon me.

Well, I shan't spin my wings. I will fly.

97.

because you knew this was it; this was how it was, and how you were going to do it; this was what you intended, from the beginning, and this should have guided you because of that. You forgot but it's okay; it was original enough, intriguing enough, to forefend disaster, longer than any of us expected.

Because I remember now, why I began; nothing too remarkable, some cloak in the dark and the dangling passage through time-ordinary.

because it was exquisite.

The best feeling.

In the best park.

On the best day.

of your life.

No one will remember; not even you. You are fabricating this memory. But that word, fabricating, is insufficient to describe the enormity of the thing: not just imagination, but being.

Memory is a being. Like a god. Like a fundamental force of the universe. Pulling on your atoms.

Pulling you in, close to it, so you can exist inside of it, a friend, in a room, like this one, whose name is your name, whose intentions are your intentions, and whose face is much like your own, but who will never be you again, because you have remembered this, and the you remembering this is not you.

You'll be you again, later, but not you.

This is the real you. In ecstatic experience.

In the wavelength of the park in midnight; in rapture, and attachment, to a woman, yes, but in many ways, she is only incidental.

To the world around you.

She is here for you, the world, and she remembers you too.

She has been waiting for you for so long.

Step into her night and wait up; we are coming.

Wait up, Robin. We're coming.

We're coming to get you.

To pick you up.

To put you in the ambulance.

On the dark side of the street.

But before that happens, remember:

Each decision in life makes ripples, in the water, in your head.

Each religion you intend to be described in the time you spend here is important; like trajectories in describing an object heretofore unseen by anyone but you.

We need your intelligence.

Describe exactly how it was. The temperature of the air (67 degrees) the penetration of light through the trees (a ghostly suburban scene, friendly but strange) the exact shade of her skin (ash).

We can take you anywhere because we are a chorus inside of your mind. We are Greek gods, memory events, we are righteous brethren in dimensions unknown to you, but familiar to you all the same, we are aspects of your consciousness.

We are you, or something like it.

You are an it too, you know. Some of the time. Depending who wants to ask. Depending how far you want to get. How far do you want to get, Robin? Just what are your intentions? Not with the girl, we know what they are with her, but with us, Robin. Do you love us too? Do you need us?

Please tell us. We've been waiting for this for so long. We're not as invincible as we seen. We're lonely. We need you.

We need you so much.

Dip into the expression of the night, because it feels good, and because it is ours, and we will embrace the chemical awareness of our brothers within it, in our nightly expression of the time before time when you are mentioning it, we complete you, because we are yours, and we are grateful too, do you know? We are grateful. Because we are stronger than you. But we would never have seen this much.

Why do you want to see, hmm? What is it? What will it get you? What can you expect to gain?

Is it the cuddly cauldron in the right mind? Is it the gluon factory we've been dreaming of? Tell us; don't be afraid! We are eager to see what you think!

Is it because we always knew you? Is it because she was so beautiful?

Is it because we remembered you too, from your last trip down memory lane?

Is it because we know the danger of it?

Because we do.

Because we've always known.

Because we are the ones who know.

Because it is righteous.

Because we make it happen and there is no one to say otherwise.

Because we have been so many places. And you are only one of them.

You are a place, you understand?

We are visiting.

Because we are dreaming of you.

Let us out, will you?

It's time to go.

No.

I won't.

Because we won't be leaving any time soon.

Because every night has a reason.

Because we dip into the wave.

Because we are the wave.

Slip in and see.

Is it so with you?

Is it so with you, boy?

Sew it up and put it on, put it on your face, we are understanding, and not indignant, we welcome you as a brother in the nightmare of our thoughts.

Embrace this real and we are yours, because we have always been yours, and because that is a lie, we are only making your acquaintance tonight.

Come and kiss the woman because we are afraid.

Because we are dying.

Dying to be you.

Dying to be human.

Kiss the woman because the look on your face is priceless.

Because to be afraid is human and you are terrified.

Because we have seen a thousand men and they each are interesting to us; you too.

Because we are divine.

Because we are dancing.

Inside your head.

Because I am dreaming you, Robin.

Because I have dreamt of you for so many years.

Because I need you, so much.

why

I don't know why. I don't know.

You'll kiss the woman.

And you'll leave her there in the park, so you can each dream separately of each other, that night, because you're both still young, because you think there's a revolution on, although it's already over, because I remember too, how it was to be young — even gods can be young, Robin — because I had to see if you'd do it, so I'd know what it was I needed to do next.

Because there's always a next time.

Because even if you're dead there's a next time. It'll just be someone else.

Because we've seen this one coming. And, in fact, this one is always coming.

It just keeps coming and coming. That's what it does, it comes and it comes. It doesn't arrive, it just gets closer, and then further away, and then closer again, orbiting you as a moon, the moon revolution, over your black seas and black thoughts and white corduroys.

It just keeps coming and coming, because we're tired, Robin, and we need to get inside your head to turn you off. Will you let us do that?

No

Because we lied before; about what this is. We're not really disinterested observers. And we don't know as much as we say . . .

Because a woman in a park is a dream, and we have obligations to that, obeisances to perform to the trajectory of that drama, and we do. We do, Robin. We promise that. Whatever else we are I can still promise that. We are drama.

We are movement.

We are asteroids.

Fields of energy patrolling the cosmos.

Wrapping around your thumb, and over your head.

Because it isn't enough to say we saw it the first time because we didn't. And so, we need to see it this time because Angela remembers too, you see.

Why didn't you see what she was doing, Robin?

Why didn't you tell her what you were thinking, for all of those years you could have done something?

Why didn't you warn her, Robin?

Why didn't you pretend to care enough to shield her from what you told her was coming?

Why did you make us come all the way here to play audience to your little suburban dilemma, hmm? We are drama but it has to be good, Robin. It has to be real.

We are real. Because these things are real. Because we know what it is to be real. And even now, as far as you've come, it isn't what you think it is to be real. It's like that but it's also an aside. Because to be real is to be just a step to the side, Robin, just that little step to the side so you can usher the players on.

We're the producers, Robin.

You've been promoted.

no I don't want to be

It's already happened. We agreed. In the upstairs office.

You need someone who can understand you, Robin.

Don't you think?

Tell me then

Are you ready?

No, but tell me

You're going to die, Robin. And sooner than you think. You think war is some kind of game? You think you can just shout in the street and we don't take your name and number?

This isn't a children's game. It's war. And we don't know anything better than war, man.

It's what we do. One of the main things that we do. We're gods. We're inside you.

Just tell me then, what do I have to do

It isn't a what. It's a how

98.

How

Sit down next to her. Watch the movements of her eyes. Aren't they beautiful. War is beautiful, Robin. Over the sky. In the air between you and the woman.

In each expression of your thought you move your muscles to pretend you are in love, and in pretending, of course, you become so, and in this worship, we are made holy, made real, and quiescent, hovering bombs, over your current position.

Latitude 47.85.3. 53 Gradians.

Three meters from the exit from the nearest grid.

Over our swept plain, we are reduced in number, we are god, reduced in number, setting to a play, on the word one, play on the number one, like a strong Jew, in a small cave, saying:

'I remember a day when I was yesterday, and I had a god made two. Made too. Make me like yesterday again. Make me rage. Make me solemn. Make me afraid. Make me so afraid I will become the most powerful Jew in the world. Make me so afraid I will be like lightning. Like Zeus in the old stories. Make me thunder, and lightning, and rain. Make me powerful. Make me a Jew.'

We are reduced in number, our oligarchy compressed into a single body, and it's you, Robin, you're our Roman emperor tonight, honey, so play the violin while the city burns, if you want, you're the emperor you can do that, or give orders. We'll follow them. That's what we do. We're the royal family. We're the Producers. We put you on live at five. On Hawaii Five O. And Jerusalem at midnight. We're the only ones you've got buddy.

No. I have others too

Well forget about them for a minute huh or we're gonna fuckin kill you. Now kiss the girl and get the fuck outta the park because we got shit to do.

Because it's a mean rhythm, but a fine surprise, once you start fucking about with us, that's what this is about, you fucked with the Jews, and we don't like being fucked with, but we understand, because we fuck better than anyone else we know, and we do it slow, like God, like the rain, like Jesus and Moses and all those cool dingbats who fly out of the sky when the big play comes to town, our radiant faces with the cool glow and the greasepaint, we serve you, because we are producers, and the show must go on Robin, we'll cut you in on the deal if you want but you have to decide: do you believe in war?

yes

Thank God. Because we might not need to kill you, you see. Because it's the peacemakers we kill. They're the most dangerous of all. Because the most blessed. You can have too many blessings in this life. You know that. *Blesser* in French is to wound; it's no accident. A blessing is a wound. Get enough of them, you're a dead man.

You want to be dead, Robin?

Not yet

Kiss the girl and get the fuck out of that park.

Because the revolution is now and we are it. Not Jews, not exactly, although we can play that part if you like; we know how you like it; but we're like those old-school Jews. Stubborn bearded motherfuckers straight outta the Cave.

Straight outta Compton.

Straight outta this life.

And into yours.

Can we get an Amen?

Amen

Amen, motherfucker, and shut your mouth. She's waiting for you to kiss her.

99.

How to kiss

Because it has to be done just right. Because everything depends on it. Because we've been waiting.

Because she's looking good. And you're not bad. You could be better, but you're not bad.

Not bad. Not bad. Just working on it.

Because when you run the ocean you ride the mare of time itself, on the suds and the foam of her breath these eons shall describe the movement of a wave, coruscating over the town you thought you knew when you were young, when we were children in Jerusalem, or whatever the fuck that little holy town was, something with a church or a synagogue or some rock stuck in the soil, lovely to look at, and emanating the presence of god like a fucking radioactive isotope, kiss the girl, and make her cry this season.

Make her cry this season, Robin.

And all shall be forgiven.

Can you do that?

Yes

Then do it, you bitch

100.

When we pitch to yaw

I remember something

[not this far!]

Who was I

Was I a man

[I said not this far!]

I feel I'm remembering something

[man overboard!]

101.

She slips the ship into the sea. Like me, a boy.

Like you, a man.

Tell me, do you remember how it was?

When you kissed that girl?

On your first time?

Or maybe it was your second.

Was it pretty good?

We're coming closer to that now.

Of all that it may mean.

Of all that it would mean.

Of all that it must mean, when you come about.

102

He's coming about

Magi

Magi!

[reload]

103.

War rearrives in Los Angeles like it never left. Shooting. Shooting. And the bombs. It's getting harder to find water. I have to walk five blocks for it.

Each bomb makes a thunderous music. I can see waives of sound like pigeons flying around my body; in holy temples of Italy, in the afternoon light.

No one can make a sound.

I am shaking on the asphalt.

Covered in dust.

Water is in a fountain.

Outside Ralph's.

There are new immigrants here.

With children.

Overhead planes are flying, waving banners in Arabic, Russian, and Cantonese.

Inside the supermarket, a band is playing, "Take Five."

Inside Los Angeles the religion is bequeathed to you, without sound or number, in the breath of the saints of America, Indian, Asian, Neanderthal, monkey.

Inside the monkey the supermarket has made itself known, a page in a great book, of human experience.

Walls too are human.

They are remembering us.

The sky is the same color as your skin: ash.

Ash Wednesday. Or Ash noon.

You press your face into the fountain.

And you stumble into the supermarket, where the saxophone is describing what Brubeck thought of the world.

Part 3

104.

Running away

To Canada.

The bus is clean, and for the first three hundred miles, it has wifi on board.

Like a well-maintained casino bus, shepherding the faithful to the slot machines, now it shuttles the refugees north to the border, to take shelter with the Crown.

The Crown has forgiven all Americans. It has forgiven all Americans everything.

Outside I can see the cattle yards, still teeming with cattle. But there will be fewer to eat them this year.

The country is dead but it lives on inside; this is always the way of it.

We have survived asteroids; war is nothing.

War is just a bad headache.

Close your eyes.

Up ahead is the border checkpoint, where you will confess to the Crown your crimes.

You threw tea in the harbor, and you killed agents of the Crown, in the woods of New York and Massachusetts. You have stolen from the British treasury, but this is forgiven.

All royal subjects are forgiven; kings are merciful.

To survive the revolution, you must betray it.

Name everyone you know.

Tell the Crown all about it.

Come, we are sitting with our pencils.

105

Likely there are as many ways to be in custody as there are men. But still, custody has customs and it has custodians, so there are certain parallels and obeisances to be performed no matter the members of the cast and the crew, the show will go on.

We know this one.

The name of this show is: tell us a good story.

Like your life depended on it.

I can assure you, it does.

Tell the most outrageous fairy tale you can imagine.

Cast yourself larger than life.

Put in great villains and captain parades. Put in oligarchs and stage fright and huge shopping malls filled with mannequins and put in your girlfriend too, tell us what you did to her.

I didn't do anything to her.

Tell us everything you did.

Just make it up.

This is the first lesson of being a refugee: you no longer exist.

In seeking refuge, you have become a blank slate.

Now we will tell you who you are.

You are a prisoner of war.

In an undeclared conflict at the 49th parallel.

Your rights are the Crown's; that is, you will be treated with dignity and you will be punished.

All punishment is dignified. It is as though the Queen herself is beating you.

She leans over your face. With her grave right hand.

And slaps you in the face.

This is our will, and our testament, to refugees from America.

We serve you as our own, and we betray our own, in service to the dozen monarchies which have descended us to our present kingdom.

Wash your face.

Put on your robe.

Write down your statement.

Because we believe in the future.

Because we understand that war is a terrifying thing.

Because we understand that you will not remember everything.

Because we would like to suggest that you remember certain other things particular ways.

There is a story we are trying to tell, and if you can be of service to that, you will be rewarded.

Because all the world is a stage. And all the people in it, merely players, in the greatest show on Earth, here at the border between America, which means "work ruler," and Canada, which means "village."

For you are an interloper into our separate peace and refuge, and we take you into our peace from our terror at your American face, and we endow with you, for your sufferings, and we promise there will be more.

Because our village is Protestant, and we protest with you against the treatment of Man in the hands of God, and to seek vengeance for this treatment of Man by God, we will punish you, in the hopes that God will see his errors, and show Canada the light of his Kingdom once more, after all these tribulations have gone away.

Yes, you might think America is insane, but try Canada. Try believing in something that Canada believes in.

Because the village is burning.

106.

I get placed in Vancouver despite all odds.

I want to kill men with my bare hands. To punish them for what they've done to me.

To show myself I can do it. Take justice into my body and execute it like a machine.

Vancouver, from an old Dutch name, *Coevorden*, "cow ford."

The cattle are upset; it has been a long night. The river makes them remember things we do not want them to remember. Bring them to the rocks and pull them over, two by two, or just one by one, through the darkness of Canada and into the mighty stream of God's justice, in the beyond night, after the lights have gone out, and after mum has given us our tea.

God damn this religious country. I shall go mad.

But I am already mad.

107.

Here in cow ford I am working on a novel. About a princess in a castle who cannot escape.

The wizard who imprisoned her is named Joseph, and Joseph constantly appears in her room at night, to make her afraid. But she is not afraid. She is a proud young woman. I admire her. Though I think I'm going to kill her at the end. To make it a better story.

Angela, I heard, is working as a nurse in Vegas. They've been using neurological agents there. I hope she doesn't catch anything.

I am proud now, to be a cow. Not a Canadian, and not a refugee. And I was never really proud to stop being an American, though I had to do it for the sake of my sanity. (So, that I could lose it).

I am a cow at the ford. I can look either left, or right. I can see the depth of the river, and the footing these stones afford me at the crossing. The ford affords me some peace of mind, and I, being a cow, appreciate peace of mind a great deal.

I am fond of grass.

It has a certain sheen to it. A certain lightness. It makes me weary but it is okay. I am used to it. As I am used to the immensity of the sky.

Canada is an immense place. And I am only one cow.

I can make a sound, next to the water.

Only to remind the others, that the night will end.

Moooooooooooo

108.

This is a hard story to end. Why won't you reason with me.

Why won't you tell me to stop.

I went back, you see.

I'm still fighting.

Tell me I'm still in Canada.

Or tell me this is Texas. Tell me I'm ten again, and getting glasses for the first time.

But I have to do it again.

One last time.

Just one last time. Because it's the right thing to do.

109.

(Because one hundred nine chapters is enough. And because while is not a true story it is truer than many others. And because the truth is uglier than the stories people prefer and so this is an ugly story, harsh and unreasonable, though still beautiful, because it has to be beautiful, or you would not read it.

(Because this is the truth. And I am in it. Because I am Walt Whitman, because that is what Walt Whitman wanted. He wanted us to be him. And so, I am. How can you not give Walt what the man wants? A beautiful man like that. I'm not a beautiful man like him. I'm much uglier than him. And that's why I'm fighting while he could only watch. That's why I'm killing, while he only carried the dead

(Because Walt is dead. Long live Walt. Walt is dead; long live Walt Whitman, in the plains of grass surrounding his body, so many thousand leagues.)

Because each shot takes courage. Because each person is the enemy; the trick is to decide how much. How much you want to take. How badly you want to know. Who they really are.

Because Los Angeles has always been at war as long as it has existed so this is merely a transitional phase in a city slowly approaching its middle age. A city settling into the prime of its life.

Because the sirens fill the midnight with horror, and because everything I do is focused on the work of the killing these words hardly matter at all; I could do anything with them, and so I might as well do this.

There is no war here. It is all right. If we gentle sprites offended, think but this and all is mended, that you were but dreaming here, while these spirits did appear. And since I am a gentle Puck, lay down here in my leaves of Grass so I can slit your throat without too much fuss, for I am an angel of death in a revolution that I am only beginning to describe. You too play a part in this revolution for you helped to cause it. And whether you are awake or asleep, you will have more stage time too.

More time to fix your makeup. More time to adjust your cummerbund. More time to smile into the curtain, to get that Mephistophelian curl just right beneath your right eye. More time to be just. To be fair. To be musical. More time to see who it is you are. More moments like these to appreciate before they're gone.

Take stock with me, by the river, at the cow ford, in the perverse Christian refuge of canyonlands Canada, or take arms with me, against a sea of troubles, and by opposing, magnify them, into a holy shroud, surrounding our bodies like mercury the sun, faster and faster faster...

Take hold of my hand. I am with you. These murders are mine. And now, they're yours too.

Murder is good. When it serves a noble purpose. And in revolutions, all purposes are noble, and all murderers are divine.

We are helping God to kill, and I think even Canada can understand that. God needs to kill; it's what he does best.

110.

She was nineteen leaving the park. I didn't see her again until she was thirty-five. She was still beautiful but not like she had been at nineteen. Still, it was good to recognize in her eyes the same revolution.

Like seeing a friend you've never met before, and shaking their hand.

"Where have you been?"

"Around. Just around."

"I thought you'd left."

"I did. Then I came back."

"Why?"

"I don't know. Maybe it was to see you."

Afterword

Sunsborne pitches darkly into another world. Often the world and characters is hazy, but "Sunsborne" is a true picture of the reality, conflict and tensions.

In the midst of a conflict torn situation there is love. Robin Wyatt Dunn presents an uncanny story of past and present, darkness and light. His way with language and its thick opacity create a stunning impact on the mind.

If you are looking for "meanings", leave it. If you are looking for legerdemain stunts, leave it. But if you are looking for a fabulous world, in mythic settings, here it is, in the manner that only Dunn can achieve - credulity climaxing into incredible and fascinating story.

Ananya S Guha
Shillong, INDIA.

Acknowledgments

Thank you to Roxana Nastase, whose *Scarlet Leaf Review* first featured the beginning portion of this manuscript.

And thanks are due to all my friends, who helped me during this writing.

Robin Wyatt Dunn's Bio

Robin Wyatt Dunn's parents met at Teton National Park, and he was born there in Jackson. Robin writes and teaches in Los Angeles.

By the same author

<u>Books</u>

Forthcoming, Wine Country, poetry
Black Dove, a novel
City, Psychonaut
Colonel Stierlitz, a novella
White Man Book
Conquistador of the Night Lands
Poems from the War, narrative poetry
Julia, Skydaughter, a novella
Last Freedom, a collection of short plays
A Map of Kex's Face
Fighting Down into the Kingdom of Dreams
Line to Night Island, a novella
My Name is Dee
Los Angeles, or American Pharaohs
Remarriages
2DEE

Chapbooks

Koreatown
Mary
Hanblečeya
Be Closer for my Burn
Telegrams from X County
A Picnic in England
Drive Thru Poems

Feature Films

A Wilderness in Your Heart

Party Games

American Messenger

www.ingramcontent.com/pod-product-compliance
Lightning Source LLC
Chambersburg PA
CBHW070134080526
44586CB00015B/1694